Dipesh Bhoir
Mumbai, Maharashtra, 401101.
ask@DipeshBhoir.com

Python101
Learning Python & Django within hours

By Dipesh Bhoir
Full-Stack Developer & Solutions Architect
with experience of coding dynamic enterprise systems at scale
for major Indian Startups & American Corporates

in partnership with Tehzeeb School
Mumbai, India.

A Tehzeeb School Original

Tehzeeb School, Mumbai.

Imprint: Independently published
ENGLISH

ISBN:	9798858226338	Hardcover edition
ISBN:	9798858221340	Paperback edition
ASIN:	B0CFZJK7JD	Hardcover
ASIN:	B0CFZFJYFR	Paperback
ASIN:	B0CG4K5SHX	Kindle

ABOUT

INDEX

Chapter	Title	Scroll
I	Introduction	8
II	Getting started with Python	13
III	Variables and Data Types	21
IV	Operators and Expressions	23
V	Control Flow	35
VI	Data Structures	38
VII	Functions	53
VIII	Modules and Packages	71
IX	Django Fundamentals	80
X	Creating a Django Project	84
XI	Building Views and Templates	88
XII	Models and Databases	92
XIII	Forms and User Input	96
XIV	User Authentication and Authorization	100
XV	Building a Complete Django Application	104
XVI	Working with Static and Media Files	108
XVII	Advanced Topics	112
XVIII	Conclusion	124

Notes

A Tehzeeb School Original

Greetings, I am Dipesh Bhoir, originally from the Mumbai-Thane region and currently based in Houston. I have experience as a full stack solutions architect, with a focus on Web technologies, Cloud computing, IoT (internet of things), IAC (infrastructure as code), CI/CD pipelines (Lean, Agile, Waterfall) and cost optimization at scale. To provide some context, my professional journey has involved collaborating with both American enterprises and Indian startup ventures, allowing me to gain valuable insights into the intricacies of both landscapes.

From an early age, my passion for computers has remained fervent. Despite a modest childhood in many aspects, my profound affinity for technology sets me apart. During my formative years, I engaged extensively in electronics assembly. Remarkably, by the age of nine, I had commenced selling computers to finance my unconventional pursuits. By the time I reached twelve, I had acquired proficiency in more than fourteen programming languages. My disposition is marked by an inherent curiosity that often diverges from conventional norms, thriving in environments that may be resistant to my presence.

My upbringing was tinged with a sense of parental detachment, leading my grandparents to assume caregiving responsibilities for a significant duration. As a result, my childhood was colored by adversity. In times of challenge, I sustained myself by crafting portfolio websites. Throughout this journey, I sought solace in technology as an avenue of escape from my circumstances. It embraced me when the world turned away.

I have made substantial contributions to diverse projects across various companies and communities, some of which may resonate with you. This account represents my effort to offer a glimpse into my background and foster a greater understanding and appreciation for the world of programming languages.

Python101 is designed for my younger-self to shrink years of concept building with structured brainstorming notes on practical implementation. If you hold this book, it's meant for one's own bloodline. The words are sacred and narratives instill character.

Keep up
DipeshBhoir.com

LinkedIn @dipeshbhoir
Twitter @thinkxis
Youtube @thinkxis
Instagram @thinkxis
Medium @thinkxis
VKontakte @thinkxis

Learn Python

A programming language designed for readability

A Tehzeeb School Original

Epistle

A Tehzeeb School Original

Programming languages are the building blocks of the digital age, enabling us to bring our ideas to life through the power of code. Among these languages, Python shines as a versatile, beginner-friendly, and widely-used choice, while Django provides a robust framework for creating web applications with ease. This book is your gateway to mastering both Python and Django, regardless of your prior coding experience.

Why Learn Python and Django?

In a landscape where technology continues to shape our world, programming languages like Python and frameworks like Django have emerged as dynamic tools that drive innovation and shape the digital future. But why should you invest your time in learning Python and Django? Let's explore the compelling reasons that make these technologies indispensable.

- Python: A Language of Simplicity and Power

Python has emerged as a language of choice for beginners and experts alike due to its intuitive syntax and extensive libraries. Its readability makes it an excellent starting point for those new to programming, while its versatility suits a wide range of applications, from web development to data analysis, artificial intelligence, scientific research, and more.

1. Ease of Learning: Python's syntax is designed for human readability, making it an excellent choice for beginners. Its simplicity allows new programmers to grasp concepts quickly and focus on problem-solving.

2. Versatility: Python is a versatile language that serves a wide range of applications. From web development to scientific computing, data analysis, machine learning, and more, Python's flexibility ensures it has a place in nearly every field.

3. Vast Ecosystem: Python boasts a rich ecosystem of libraries and frameworks that accelerate development. Whether you're building a website, working with data, or exploring artificial intelligence, chances are there's a Python library to assist you.

4. Community and Support: Python has a thriving global community of developers who contribute to its growth. This community offers a wealth of resources, tutorials, and forums for troubleshooting, making your learning journey smoother.

- Django: Empowering Web Development

Django, built on the foundation of Python, is a web framework designed to simplify the complexities of web development. Its "batteries-included" philosophy equips developers with pre-built components, allowing you to focus on crafting the unique aspects of your application. By learning Django, you'll gain the skills to create dynamic, interactive, and secure web experiences.

INTRODUCTION

1. Rapid Development:
Django's philosophy of "batteries included" means you have access to a plethora of pre-built components. This accelerates development and empowers you to focus on crafting unique aspects of your application.

2. Clean and Maintainable Code:
Django enforces a clean and consistent coding style, which promotes maintainability and collaboration among developers. This structure makes it easier to work on projects of varying sizes.

3. Security:
Security is paramount in web development. Django incorporates built-in security features to safeguard against common web vulnerabilities, helping you build robust and secure applications.

4. Scalability:
As your application grows, Django's scalability features allow you to efficiently handle increased traffic and demand. This ensures your application can evolve without sacrificing performance.

-   Why This Combination Matters
The synergy between Python and Django creates a powerful development ecosystem that streamlines the creation of web applications:

1. Efficiency:
Python's concise syntax and Django's comprehensive framework reduce the amount of code you need to write, saving time and effort.

2. Learning Curve:
If you're new to programming, Python's readability and simplicity will ease your entry into the coding world. As you master Python, Django's user-friendly structure will help you transition into web development smoothly.

3. Career Opportunities:
Proficiency in Python and Django opens doors to a variety of job opportunities, from web developer to data analyst, machine learning engineer, and more. These skills are in demand across industries.

4. Innovation:
Python's versatility and Django's robustness encourage creativity. You can bring your unique ideas to life, whether it's a dynamic website, an interactive application, or a data-driven project.

Learning Python and Django isn't just about coding—it's about gaining the ability to shape technology and create meaningful digital experiences. The skills you acquire will empower you to innimate, solve problems, and contribute to a rapidly evolving technological landscape. As we journey through this book, you'll unlock the potential of these technologies, expanding your horizons and embarking on an exciting adventure of creativity and discovery.

Who Is This Book For?
Whether you're a complete novice or a seasoned programmer, this book is designed to accelerate your Python and Django learning curve. If you're new to programming, you'll find a welcoming entry point that gradually guides you through fundamental concepts. For experienced developers, we offer insights into Python's nuances and Django's best practices.

How Is This Book Structured?
This book is divided into three parts, each building upon the previous one:

Part I - Python Basics:
Lay the groundwork with Python's syntax, data types, control flow, and functions.

Part II - Django Fundamentals:
Explore Django's MVC architecture, views, models, forms, authentication, and more.

Part III - Advanced Topics:
Dive into RESTful APIs, testing, debugging, deployment, and scaling.

Setting Up Your Development Environment
Before we delve into the exciting world of Python and Django, it's essential to ensure that your development environment is properly set up. A well-configured environment will enable you to write, test, and run your code smoothly. In this chapter, we'll guide you through the process of setting up both Python and Django, step by step.

Installing Python
Python comes in different versions, but for this book, we'll focus on Python 3. Python 3 is the latest iteration of the language and offers numerous improvements over its predecessor, Python 2. Follow these steps to install Python 3 on your system:

1. Choose Your Operating System: Visit the official Python website (python.org) and navigate to the "Downloads" section. Select the appropriate installer for your operating system (Windows, macOS, or Linux).

2. Run the Installer: Once the installer is downloaded, run it and follow the installation prompts. Make sure to check the option that adds Python to your system's PATH environment variable. This will allow you to run Python from any location in the command prompt or terminal.

3. Verify Installation: To verify that Python is installed correctly, open a terminal or command prompt and type python3 --version (on some systems, it might be just python --version). You should see the installed Python version displayed.

Installing Django
With Python installed, you're ready to move on to Django, the powerful web framework that leverages Python's capabilities for web development. Here's how to get Django up and running:

1. Install Django: Open your terminal or command prompt and type the following command:

```
pip install django
```

Pip is the package installer for Python, and it will download and install Django along with its dependencies.

2. Verify Django Installation: After installation is complete, you can verify that Django is installed by running:

```
python -m django --version
```

This command will display the installed Django version.

Creating a Virtual Environment (Optional but Recommended)
Python's virtual environments allow you to isolate project-specific dependencies, preventing conflicts between different projects. To create a virtual environment, follow these steps:

3. Install Virtualenv: If you haven't already, install the virtualenv package using pip:

pip install virtualenv

4. Create a Virtual Environment: Navigate to your project directory in the terminal and create a virtual environment by running:

virtualenv venv

This will create a folder named venv containing the isolated environment.

Activate the Virtual Environment: Activate the virtual environment by running the appropriate command based on your operating system:

-   On Windows: venv\Scripts\activate
-   On macOS and Linux: source venv/bin/activate

With your virtual environment active, any packages you install using pip will only affect this specific project, keeping your global Python environment clean.

Congratulations! You've successfully set up your development environment for Python and Django. You're now equipped with the tools you need to begin your coding journey. In the upcoming chapters, we'll start exploring the fundamental concepts of Python and gradually transition to building web applications using Django. Get ready to write your first lines of code and witness your creations come to life!

Let's Begin the Journey
As you embark on this journey, remember that learning to code is an adventure of discovery and problem-solving. Embrace challenges, experiment with code, and don't hesitate to seek help when needed. Let your curiosity guide you, and soon you'll wield the power to create applications that enrich the digital landscape.
Are you ready to unlock the world of Python and Django? Let's start coding!

INTRODUCTION

Getting Started with Python
- History of Python
- Installing Python
- Your First Python Program
- Understanding the Python Interpreter

Python is often referred to as a "programming language for everyone" due to its user-friendly syntax and versatility. In this part, we'll start from the ground up, introducing you to the basics of Python programming. By the end of this section, you'll have a solid foundation to build upon as you explore more advanced concepts.

Part I: Learn Python

- History of Python

In the ever-evolving landscape of programming languages, Python stands out as a versatile, readable, and powerful language that has captivated developers, educators, and businesses around the world. The history of Python is a fascinating journey through the collaborative efforts of its creators, the community that nurtured it, and its widespread adoption in various domains.

The Birth of Python

Python's story begins in the late 1980s with a Dutch programmer named Guido van Rossum. Guido was working at the Centrum Wiskunde & Informatica (CWI) in the Netherlands, a research institute where he was part of a team developing a language called ABC. ABC was intended to be an easy-to-read language for non-programmers, but it faced limitations in terms of extensibility and practicality.

Guido van Rossum, frustrated with the shortcomings of ABC, set out to create a new language that would combine the ease of use with the power of extensibility. In December 1989, during his Christmas holidays, Guido started working on his project, which he later named Python, inspired by his love for the British comedy group Monty Python.

Python was designed to be a general-purpose programming language with a focus on simplicity and readability. Guido's goals included:

- A clean and easy-to-read syntax, emphasizing code readability.
- Support for multiple programming paradigms, including procedural, object-oriented, and functional programming.
- A comprehensive standard library to simplify common tasks.
- Extensibility through modules and libraries.
- An interpreter that could run code interactively, which was a novel concept at the time.

Python's Early Years

Python's development progressed steadily throughout the early 1990s. Guido released Python's first public version, Python 0.9.0, in February 1991. This version already included features that would become staples of the language, such as exception handling, functions, and modules.

Python's early adopters were primarily in the scientific and academic communities, drawn to its simplicity and readability. Its use cases expanded to include tasks like automating repetitive processes, data analysis, and prototyping.

In 1994, Python 1.0 was released, marking an important milestone. This version included features like lambda, map, filter, and reduce, further enhancing Python's capabilities.

Python 2.x and the Rise in Popularity

Python 2.0 was released in October 2000, bringing a garbage collector, Unicode support, and list comprehensions. The early 2000s saw Python's popularity grow steadily, as it gained a reputation for being a versatile language suitable for a wide range of applications.

Part I: Learn Python

Python's simplicity and readability made it a top choice for teaching programming. Many universities and educational institutions adopted Python as a beginner-friendly language. Additionally, its use in web development started to gain traction with frameworks like Zope and Django.

Python 3.x: A Modernization Effort

As Python continued to evolve, some challenges emerged. One significant issue was the coexistence of two major Python branches: Python 2.x and Python 3.x. Python 3 was introduced in December 2008 as an effort to address some fundamental issues and make the language more consistent and modern.

However, the transition from Python 2 to Python 3 proved to be more complex than initially anticipated. Python 3 introduced backward-incompatible changes to the language, which meant that code written for Python 2 wouldn't necessarily work in Python 3 without modifications. This created a divide in the Python community, with some developers choosing to stick with Python 2 for various reasons.

Python Today: A Global Community

Despite the challenges of the Python 2 to Python 3 transition, Python's popularity continued to soar. Python is now one of the most widely used programming languages globally. Its use spans various domains:

- Web Development: Frameworks like Flask and Django are immensely popular for building web applications.

- Data Science: Python is the go-to language for data analysis, machine learning, and artificial intelligence, with libraries such as NumPy, pandas, and TensorFlow.

- Automation: Python's simplicity makes it ideal for automating tasks, from scripting to system administration.

- Education: Python remains a favorite in academia for teaching programming and computer science concepts.

The Future of Python

Python's journey is far from over. The Python Software Foundation (PSF), a non-profit organization, oversees the development of Python, ensuring its stability and growth. Python continues to evolve, with regular releases introducing new features and improvements.

As the programming world continues to change, Python adapts, making it a language that stands the test of time. Its thriving community of developers, educators, and enthusiasts ensures that Python remains a powerful and accessible tool for years to come.

Part I: Learn Python

- Installing Python

To begin your Python journey, you'll need to install the language on your computer. Follow the instructions provided at the beginning to install Python on your preferred operating system. Once you're set up, you can move on to writing your first Python program.

Essential Python Packages: A Guide to Useful pip Installations

Python's power lies not only in its simplicity but also in its extensibility. The Python Package Index (PyPI) hosts a vast ecosystem of libraries and packages that can significantly enhance your Python programming experience. This chapter is a curated list of essential Python packages, each serving a unique purpose and providing valuable tools for various tasks. To install these packages, use the pip package manager.

Installing Packages with pip

Before diving into the list, let's briefly review how to use pip to install packages. Open your command-line interface and run the following command:

pip install package-name

Replace package-name with the name of the package you want to install. pip will automatically download and install the package and its dependencies.

Upgrading Packages

You can also use pip to upgrade packages to their latest versions:

pip install --upgrade package-name

Now, let's explore some of the most useful Python packages:

NumPy

Purpose: NumPy is the fundamental package for scientific computing with Python. It provides support for large, multi-dimensional arrays and matrices, along with a collection of mathematical functions to operate on these arrays.
Installation:
pip install numpy

pandas

Purpose: pandas is a powerful data manipulation and analysis library. It provides data structures like DataFrames and Series, making it easy to work with structured data, including CSV and Excel files.
Installation:
pip install pandas

Matplotlib
Purpose: Matplotlib is a popular data visualization library that allows you to create a wide range of static, animated, or interactive plots and graphs.
Installation:
pip install matplotlib

Requests
Purpose: The requests library simplifies HTTP requests in Python. It is commonly used for sending HTTP GET and POST requests, making it essential for web scraping and interacting with web APIs.
pip install requests

Flask
Purpose: Flask is a micro web framework for building web applications in Python. It is simple and easy to use, making it an excellent choice for web development beginners.
Installation:
pip install flask

Django
Purpose: Django is a high-level web framework for building robust and scalable web applications. It follows the "batteries-included" philosophy, providing many built-in features for common web development tasks.
Installation:
pip install django

SQLAlchemy
Purpose: SQLAlchemy is a powerful and flexible Object-Relational Mapping (ORM) library. It simplifies database interaction by allowing you to work with databases in a Pythonic way.
Installation:
pip install sqlalchemy

Scikit Learn
Purpose: scikit-learn is a machine learning library that provides simple and efficient tools for data analysis and modeling. It includes various algorithms for classification, regression, clustering, and more.

Installation:

pip install scikit-learn

Part I: Learn Python

TensorFlow
Purpose: TensorFlow is an open-source machine learning framework developed by Google. It is widely used for building and training deep neural networks for tasks such as image classification and natural language processing.

Installation:

pip install tensorflow

pytest
Purpose: pytest is a testing framework that simplifies the process of writing and executing unit tests in Python. It is known for its simplicity and extensibility.

Installation:

pip install pytest

Jupyter Notebook
Purpose: Jupyter Notebook is an interactive web-based environment for creating and sharing documents that contain live code, equations, visualizations, and narrative text. It is widely used in data science and education.

Installation:

pip install jupyter

Beautiful Soup
Purpose: Beautiful Soup is a library for web scraping HTML and XML documents. It provides tools for parsing and navigating HTML, making it easier to extract data from web pages.

Installation:

pip install beautifulsoup4

pytest-cov
Purpose: pytest-cov is a plugin for pytest that measures code coverage during testing. It helps you identify which parts of your code are covered by tests and which are not.

Installation:

pip install pytest-cov

Part I: Learn Python

Flask-RESTful
Purpose: Flask-RESTful is an extension for Flask that simplifies the creation of RESTful APIs. It provides tools for defining resources and handling HTTP methods like GET, POST, PUT, and DELETE.

Installation:

pip install flask-restful

pytz
Purpose: pytz is a library for working with time zones in Python. It provides extensive support for converting between time zones and handling daylight saving time.
Installation:
pip install pytz

Pillow
Purpose: Pillow is a powerful image processing library that allows you to open, manipulate, and save various image file formats. It is particularly useful for tasks like resizing, cropping, and adding filters to images.

Installation:

pip install pillow

This chapter has provided you with a comprehensive list of essential Python packages that can greatly enhance your development and data analysis capabilities. The Python ecosystem is rich with libraries, so explore and discover additional packages that suit your specific needs as you continue your Python journey. Remember to keep your packages updated for access to the latest features and improvements.

- Your First Python Program

Let's write a simple "Hello, World!" program to get you started

print("Hello, World!")

To run this program, open a text editor, paste the code, and save the file with a .py extension (e.g., hello.py). Then, open your terminal or command prompt, navigate to the directory where you saved the file, and run:

python hello.py

You should see the text "Hello, World!" displayed on your screen.

- Understanding the Python Interpreter

Python's interactive mode and the Python interpreter provide a convenient way to write and execute code line by line, making it an excellent tool for learning, testing, and experimenting with Python code. In this chapter, we'll explore how to use the Python interpreter and its interactive mode.

Launching the Python Interpreter

To start the Python interpreter, open your terminal or command prompt and type python. This will launch the Python interpreter, and you should see a prompt that looks something like this:

Python 3.9.6 (default, Jul 28 2021, 17:14:49)
[GCC 9.3.0] on linux
Type "help", "copyright", "credits" or "license" for more information.
>>>

Now you can begin typing Python code directly and see the results immediately.

Interactive Mode Examples

Let's explore some examples of using the Python interpreter in interactive mode:

Basic Arithmetic:
You can perform arithmetic operations directly in the interpreter:
>>> 2 + 3
5

Printing Messages:
You can use the print() function to display messages:
>>> print("Hello from the interpreter!")
Hello from the interpreter!
Exiting the Interpreter:
To exit the Python interpreter, simply type exit():
>>> exit()

Practical Applications

The Python interpreter's interactive mode is beneficial for various purposes:

- Learning: It's an excellent environment for learning Python because you can experiment with code in real-time.

- Testing: You can quickly test code snippets or small pieces of functionality without creating entire scripts or programs.

Part I: Learn Python

- Debugging: The interactive mode can be used for debugging and exploring variables and data structures during development.

In the upcoming chapters, we'll dive deeper into Python's fundamental concepts, including variables, data types, operators, control flow, functions, and more. As you progress through these topics, you'll build a strong understanding of Python's building blocks, setting the stage for more complex programming tasks. Get ready to embark on a coding journey that will empower you to create, innovate, and problem-solve with Python!

Variables and Data Types
- Naming Variables
- Numeric Data Types (int, float)
- Text Data Type (str)
- Boolean Data Type (bool)
- Type Conversion

In the world of Python and Django development, understanding variables and data types is your first step towards harnessing the power of these dynamic programming languages. Variables allow you to store and manipulate data, while data types define the nature of that data, such as numbers, text, or collections. In this chapter, we'll embark on a journey to explore the fundamental concepts of variables and data types in Python. By the end of this exploration, you'll be well-equipped to declare variables, assign values, and work with various data types, setting the foundation for building dynamic and data-driven applications using Django. So, let's dive into the core of Python programming and grasp the essentials of variables and data types.

In this chapter, we'll dive into the fundamentals of variables and data types in Python. Understanding these concepts is crucial as they form the building blocks of any programming language.

- Naming Variables

Variables are containers for storing data values. To create a variable, you need to choose a name for it. Here are some rules for naming variables:

- Variable names can consist of letters, numbers, and underscores.
- They must start with a letter or an underscore (not a number).
- Variable names are case-sensitive, meaning myVar and myvar are treated as distinct variables.
- Avoid using Python's reserved words (like if, for, while, etc.) as variable names.

Example:
name = "John"
age = 25

- Numeric Data Types (int, float)

Python supports two main numeric data types:
1. int: Represents integers (whole numbers) like -3, 0, 42.
2. float: Represents floating-point numbers (decimals) like -1.5, 3.14, 0.0.

Example:
my_int = 7
my_float = 3.14

- Text Data Type (str)

Strings are used to represent text in Python. They are enclosed in either single or double quotation marks.

Example:
greeting = "Hello, world!"

- Boolean Data Type (bool)

Boolean values represent two states: True or False. They are often used in conditional statements and logical operations.

Example:

is_ready = True
is_open = False

- Type Conversion

Python allows you to convert between different data types. For example, you can convert an integer to a float, or a string to an integer.

Example:

```
# Converting int to float
my_int = 5
my_float = float(my_int) # my_float will be 5.0

# Converting string to int
my_string = "10"
my_int = int(my_string) # my_int will be 10
```

Understanding variables and data types is crucial because they determine how you manipulate and work with information in your programs. As you progress, you'll find yourself working with various data types and using them to build more complex and dynamic applications. With a solid grasp of these foundational concepts, you're well on your way to becoming proficient in Python programming.

Operators and Expressions
- Arithmetic Operators
- Comparison Operators
- Logical Operators
- Operator Precedence

Operators and expressions are the building blocks of Python programming, enabling you to perform a wide range of operations on your data. Whether you're working with numbers, strings, or other data types, understanding how to use operators and create expressions is essential for manipulating and analyzing your data effectively. In this chapter, we'll embark on a journey to explore the world of operators and expressions in Python. We'll cover arithmetic, comparison, logical operators, as well as the creation of complex expressions. This knowledge forms the bedrock for crafting dynamic algorithms and solving real-world problems with Python and Django. So, let's dive into the realm of operators and expressions, and empower your Python coding endeavors.

In the world of programming, operators play a crucial role in performing various operations on data. In this chapter, we'll explore different types of operators and how they work within Python. Specifically, we'll delve into arithmetic, comparison, logical operators, and operator precedence.

- Arithmetic Operators

Arithmetic operators are used to perform mathematical calculations. Here are some common arithmetic operators in Python:

- Addition: +
- Subtraction: -
- Multiplication: *
- Division: /
- Modulus (remainder): %
- Exponentiation: **
- Floor Division: //

Arithmetic operators in Python are fundamental for performing various mathematical calculations within your programs. In this chapter, we will explore the common arithmetic operators in Python and provide examples of their usage.

For example:
```
x = 10
y = 3

print(x + y) # Output: 13
print(x * y) # Output: 30
print(x / y) # Output: 3.333...
print(x % y) # Output: 1
print(x ** y) # Output: 1000
print(x // y) # Output: 3
```

Common Arithmetic Operators
Addition (+)
The addition operator (+) is used to add two or more numbers together.
```
x = 10
y = 3

result = x + y
print(result)  # Output: 13
```

Subtraction (-)
The subtraction operator (-) is used to subtract the right operand from the left operand.
```
x = 10
y = 3
```

```python
result = x - y
print(result)  # Output: 7
```

Multiplication (*)
The multiplication operator (*) is used to multiply two or more numbers.
```python
x = 10
y = 3
```

```python
result = x * y
print(result)  # Output: 30
```

Division (/)
The division operator (/) is used to divide the left operand by the right operand, and it returns a floating-point result.
```python
x = 10
y = 3
```

```python
result = x / y
print(result)  # Output: 3.333...
```

Modulus (remainder) (%)
The modulus operator (%) is used to find the remainder when the left operand is divided by the right operand.
```python
x = 10
y = 3
```

```python
result = x % y
print(result)  # Output: 1
```

Exponentiation (**)
The exponentiation operator (**) is used to raise the left operand to the power of the right operand.
```python
x = 10
y = 3
```

```python
result = x ** y
print(result)  # Output: 1000
```

Floor Division (//)
The floor division operator (//) is used to perform division that rounds down to the nearest integer.
```python
x = 10
y = 3
```

```python
result = x // y
print(result)  # Output: 3
```

Practical Applications

Arithmetic operators are essential for a wide range of applications, including:

- Financial calculations
- Data analysis and manipulation
- Game development for scoring and calculations
- Scientific computing for mathematical modeling\

Understanding how to use these operators effectively is crucial for performing various mathematical operations in your Python programs.

we've explored the common arithmetic operators in Python and provided examples of their usage. These operators are fundamental for performing mathematical calculations in Python and are widely used in various programming domains.

- Comparison Operators

Comparison operators are used to compare values. They return True or False based on whether the comparison is true or false. Here are some common comparison operators:

- Equal to: ==
- Not equal to: !=
- Greater than: >
- Less than: <
- Greater than or equal to: >=
- Less than or equal to: <=

For example:

```
a = 5
b = 8

print(a == b) # Output: False
print(a != b) # Output: True
print(a > b) # Output: False
print(a < b) # Output: True
```

- Logical Operators

Logical operators are used to combine conditional statements. They include and, or, and not.

- and: Returns True if both conditions are true.
- or: Returns True if at least one condition is true.
- not: Returns the opposite boolean value.

For example:

```
p = True
q = False

print(p and q) # Output: False
print(p or q) # Output: True
print(not p) # Output: False
```

Logical operators in Python are used to combine or manipulate conditional statements. These operators, which include and, or, and not, are essential for controlling the flow of your program based on various conditions. In this chapter, we'll explore the common logical operators in Python and provide examples of their usage.

Common Logical Operators
and Operator
The and operator returns True if both of its operands (conditions) are True. Otherwise, it returns False.

```
p = True
q = False

result = p and q
print(result)  # Output: False
```

or Operator
The or operator returns True if at least one of its operands (conditions) is True. It returns False only if both operands are False.

```
p = True
q = False

result = p or q
print(result)  # Output: True
```

not Operator

Part I: Learn Python

The not operator returns the opposite boolean value of its operand. If the operand is True, it returns False, and vice versa.

```python
p = True

result = not p
print(result)  # Output: False
```

Practical Applications

Logical operators are essential for decision-making and flow control in your Python programs. They are commonly used in scenarios such as:

- Conditional Statements: if, elif, and else statements use logical operators to determine which code block to execute.

- Filtering Data: Logical operators are used to filter data based on multiple conditions in data analysis and processing tasks.

- User Authentication: Logical operators can be used to check if a user's input matches specific criteria for authentication.

we've explored the common logical operators in Python: and, or, and not. Understanding how to use these operators effectively is crucial for creating conditional statements and controlling the flow of your Python programs. Logical operators provide the foundation for making decisions and implementing complex logic in your code.

- Operator Precedence

Operator precedence in Python determines the order in which operations are performed within an expression. Understanding operator precedence is crucial because it ensures that expressions are evaluated correctly. In this chapter, we'll explore how operator precedence works in Python and how you can use parentheses to override the default order of operations.

Understanding Operator Precedence

Python follows a specific set of rules for operator precedence, similar to mathematics. Some operators have higher precedence than others, meaning they are evaluated first. Here are some common operators and their precedence levels, from highest to lowest:

Exponentiation (**)

Multiplication (*), Division (/), Floor Division (//), Modulus (%)

Addition (+) and Subtraction (-)

Comparisons (<, <=, >, >=, ==, !=)

Logical NOT (not)

Logical AND (and)

Logical OR (or)

For example, in the expression 2 + 3 * 4, the multiplication (*) is performed before addition (+), resulting in the output 14.

Using Parentheses to Override Precedence

You can use parentheses to explicitly specify the order of operations in an expression, just like in mathematics. Anything enclosed in parentheses is evaluated first.

```
result = (2 + 3) * 4
print(result)  # Output: 20
```

In this example, the addition within the parentheses is evaluated before the multiplication, resulting in the output 20.

Practical Applications

Understanding operator precedence is essential for writing correct and predictable Python code. It is particularly important in complex mathematical or logical expressions, such as those used in scientific calculations, data analysis, and programming puzzles.

we've explored operator precedence in Python, which determines the order in which operations are performed within an expression. By mastering operator precedence and using parentheses when needed, you can ensure that your Python code evaluates expressions correctly and produces the expected results. This knowledge is valuable when working with complex expressions and mathematical computations in your Python programs.

Control Flow
- Conditional Statements (if, elif, else)
- Loops (for, while)
- Control Flow Examples

Control flow structures are the navigational tools that steer the execution of your Python and Django programs. They allow you to make decisions, repeat actions, and create flexible, dynamic workflows. In this chapter, we'll embark on a journey to explore the world of control flow in Python. From conditional statements like if and else to loops like for and while, you'll discover how to control the flow of your code and make it responsive to different situations. Mastering control flow is crucial for creating algorithms, handling user input, and building robust, interactive web applications using Django. So, let's dive into the realm of control flow and equip you with the skills to shape your Python programs according to your needs.

Control flow structures are essential tools for directing the flow of your program's execution. In this chapter, we'll delve into two fundamental control flow mechanisms in Python: conditional statements and loops.

- Conditional Statements (if, elif, else)

Conditional statements allow your program to make decisions based on conditions. The if statement is at the heart of this mechanism, and it can be expanded with elif (short for "else if") and else clauses. Here's an example:

```
age = 20

if age < 18:
print("You're a minor.")
elif age >= 18 and age < 65:
print("You're an adult.")
else:
print("You're a senior citizen.")
```

In this example, the program evaluates the age and prints a message based on the condition met.

o Loops (for, while)

Loops enable your program to execute a block of code repeatedly. Python offers two primary loop structures: the for loop and the while loop.

For Loop:

The for loop iterates over a sequence (such as a list, tuple, or range) and executes a block of code for each item in the sequence. Here's a simple example:

```
fruits = ["apple", "banana", "cherry"]
for fruit in fruits:
print(fruit)
```

While Loop:

The while loop continues executing a block of code as long as a specified condition remains true. Be cautious to include a condition that eventually becomes false, or the loop could run indefinitely. Here's an example:

```
count = 0
while count < 5:
print("Count is:", count)
count += 1
```

Part I: Learn Python

- Control Flow Examples

Let's tie everything together with a control flow example. Suppose you want to calculate the sum of even numbers between 1 and 10 using a loop:

```python
sum_even = 0
for num in range(1, 11):
if num % 2 == 0:
sum_even += num

print("Sum of even numbers:", sum_even)
```

In this example, the for loop iterates over the numbers from 1 to 10, and the if statement checks if each number is even. If it is, the number is added to the sum_even variable.

Understanding control flow is crucial for making your programs responsive and adaptable. As you practice conditional statements and loops, you'll gain the ability to create dynamic applications that adjust their behavior based on input and conditions. This is a pivotal skill that forms the basis for more complex programming tasks you'll encounter as you continue your Python journey.

Data Structures
- Lists
- Tuples
- Dictionaries
- Sets

Data structures are the bedrock of efficient and organized data management in Python and Django applications. They enable you to store, retrieve, and manipulate data with precision and speed. In this chapter, we'll embark on a journey through the world of data structures, exploring key concepts such as lists, tuples, dictionaries, sets, and more. By understanding these data structures and their properties, you'll gain the tools to organize and work with data effectively, whether you're building a web application with Django or solving complex computational problems in Python. So, let's dive into the realm of data structures and unlock the potential of structured data handling in your Python and Django projects.

In the world of programming, lists are like containers that hold a collection of items. These items can be of any data type, such as numbers, strings, or even other lists. Lists are a fundamental data structure in Python, offering versatility and flexibility for various tasks.

- Lists

Creating a List

To create a list in Python, enclose the items in square brackets [] and separate them with commas. Here's an example:

fruits = ["apple", "banana", "orange", "grape"]

Accessing List Items

You can access individual items in a list by their index. Python uses zero-based indexing, meaning the first item is at index 0, the second item is at index 1, and so on. For example:

first_fruit = fruits[0] # Accesses the first item ("apple")
second_fruit = fruits[1] # Accesses the second item ("banana")

Modifying List Items

Lists are mutable, which means you can modify their contents after creation. To change an item at a specific index, simply assign a new value to that index:

fruits[2] = "pear" # Replaces "orange" with "pear"

Adding and Removing Items

You can append items to the end of a list using the append() method:

fruits.append("kiwi") # Adds "kiwi" to the end of the list

To remove an item by value, you can use the remove() method:

fruits.remove("banana") # Removes the item "banana"

List Slicing

You can create sublists by using slicing. Slicing allows you to extract a portion of the list. For example:

selected_fruits = fruits[1:3] # Creates a new list with items at index 1 and 2

Common List Methods

- len(list): Returns the number of items in the list.
- list.append(item): Adds the item to the end of the list.
- list.insert(index, item): Inserts the item at the specified index.
- list.pop(index): Removes and returns the item at the specified index.
- item in list: Checks if an item exists in the list.

Lists are versatile and powerful tools for storing and manipulating data. They're widely used in various programming scenarios, such as managing collections of data, implementing algorithms, and more. As you explore programming with Python, understanding how to work with lists will become an invaluable skill in your toolkit.

Using len(list) to Determine the Number of Items in a List
In Java Spring Boot, working with lists is a common task in application development. Lists are used to store collections of items, and it's often essential to know how many items are present in a list. To achieve this, you can use the len(list) method. In this chapter, we'll explore how to use len(list) effectively to count the number of items in a list and discuss practical use cases.

Introduction to len(list)
The len(list) method is a built-in function in Java that allows you to determine the number of items, or elements, present in a list. It is a straightforward and efficient way to obtain the size or length of a list, which can be crucial when working with data structures and collections. In Spring Boot, this method is readily available for use with Java's standard libraries.

Syntax
int size = list.size();

Example Usage
```java
import java.util.ArrayList;
import java.util.List;

public class ListLengthExample {
    public static void main(String[] args) {
        List<String> fruits = new ArrayList<>();

        fruits.add("Apple");
        fruits.add("Banana");
        fruits.add("Orange");

        int size = fruits.size();

        System.out.println("The number of fruits in the list is: " + size);
    }
}
```

Practical Applications

1. Data Validation

You can use len(list) to check if a list contains the expected number of elements. For instance, in a Spring Boot web application form, you may want to validate if all required fields have been filled out before processing the form.

2. Loop Iteration
Knowing the length of a list is essential when iterating through its elements using loops. You can use a for loop to iterate through each item in the list, and the length obtained from len(list) determines the number of iterations.

3. Resource Management
In Spring Boot, managing resources, such as database connections or thread pools, may involve keeping track of how many resources are in use. len(list) can help maintain resource pools efficiently.

Using list.append(item) to Add an Item to the End of a List
In Java Spring Boot, lists are widely used to store and manage collections of data. Often, you'll need to add new elements to a list. One common way to do this is by using the list.append(item) method. In this chapter, we'll explore how to use list.append(item) effectively to add an item to the end of a list and discuss practical use cases.

Introduction to list.append(item)
The list.append(item) method is a convenient way to add an item to the end of an existing list. This is particularly useful when you want to dynamically grow a list by adding new elements without specifying an index. In Spring Boot, you can use this method with Java's standard libraries to work with lists effectively.

Syntax
list.add(item);

Example Usage

```
import java.util.ArrayList;
import java.util.List;

public class ListAppendExample {
    public static void main(String[] args) {
        List<String> fruits = new ArrayList<>();

        fruits.add("Apple");
        fruits.add("Banana");
```

```
    fruits.add("Orange");

    System.out.println("The updated list of fruits is: " + fruits);
  }
}
```

Practical Applications

1. User Input Handling
When developing Spring Boot applications that involve user input, you can use list.append(item) to add user-submitted data to a list. For example, when creating a to-do list application, new tasks can be appended to a list as they are created.

2. Dynamic Data Storage
In scenarios where data is continuously generated or received, such as log entries in a web application, using list.append(item) ensures that new data is added to the end of the list, preserving the chronological order of entries.

3. Building Dynamic Lists
In user interfaces, you might need to create lists that expand as users interact with the application. list.append(item) is a fundamental

Using list.insert(index, item) to Insert an Item at a Specified Index
In Java Spring Boot, working with lists often involves the need to insert an item at a specific position within the list. This can be achieved using the list.insert(index, item) method. In this chapter, we'll explore how to use list.insert(index, item) effectively to insert an item at a specified index in a list and discuss practical use cases.

Introduction to list.insert(index, item)
The list.insert(index, item) method is a powerful way to add an item to a list at a precise location, determined by the specified index. This allows you to control the exact position where the new element should be placed within the list. In Spring Boot, you can use this method with Java's standard libraries to manipulate lists efficiently.

Syntax
list.add(index, item);

Example Usage
import java.util.ArrayList;
import java.util.List;

Part I: Learn Python

```java
public class ListInsertExample {
    public static void main(String[] args) {
        List<String> fruits = new ArrayList<>();

        fruits.add("Apple");
        fruits.add("Banana");
        fruits.add("Orange");

        fruits.add(1, "Mango");

        System.out.println("The updated list of fruits is: " + fruits);
    }
}
```

Practical Applications

1. Reordering Items
list.insert(index, item) is useful when you need to change the order of items in a list. For example, in a Spring Boot e-commerce application, you may allow users to rearrange items in their shopping cart.

2. Priority Lists
In task management or project planning applications, you can use list.insert(index, item) to insert tasks or milestones at specific positions within a priority list.

3. Custom Sorting
When custom sorting is required based on certain criteria, you can use list.insert(index, item) to insert elements in a way that aligns with your sorting logic.

Using list.pop(index) to Remove and Retrieve an Item at a Specified Index
In Java Spring Boot, manipulating lists often involves the need to remove an item at a specific position and retrieve it simultaneously. The list.pop(index) method is commonly used for this purpose. In this chapter, we'll explore how to use list.pop(index) effectively to remove and return an item at a specified index in a list and discuss practical use cases.

Introduction to list.pop(index)
The list.pop(index) method is a versatile way to remove an item from a list at a precise location, determined by the specified index. Simultaneously, it returns the removed item, allowing you to process or store it as needed. In Spring Boot, you can use this method with Java's standard libraries to efficiently manipulate lists.

Syntax
Item removedItem = list.remove(index);

Example Usage
import java.util.ArrayList;
import java.util.List;

```java
public class ListPopExample {
    public static void main(String[] args) {
        List<String> fruits = new ArrayList<>();

        fruits.add("Apple");
        fruits.add("Banana");
        fruits.add("Orange");

        String removedFruit = fruits.remove(1);

        System.out.println("Removed fruit: " + removedFruit);
        System.out.println("Updated list of fruits: " + fruits);
    }
}
```

Practical Applications

1. Undo Functionality
In Spring Boot applications, you can implement undo functionality by using list.pop(index) to remove and retrieve the most recent action or state, allowing users to revert changes.

2. Managing Queues
list.pop(index) is valuable in scenarios where items are processed in a queue-like fashion. It allows you to dequeue (remove) items while simultaneously providing access to the removed item for further processing.

3. Controlled Removal
When you need to carefully control which items are removed from a list based on specific criteria, list.pop(index) can be used to ensure that only items at certain indices are removed.

Using item in list to Check if an Item Exists in a List
In Java Spring Boot, determining whether a particular item exists within a list is a common operation. This can be efficiently achieved using the item in list construct. In this chapter, we'll

Part I: Learn Python

explore how to use item in list effectively to check if an item exists in a list and discuss practical use cases.

Introduction to item in list

The item in list construct is a straightforward way to check if a specific item or element is present within a list. It provides a Boolean result, indicating whether the item is found in the list. In Spring Boot, you can use this construct with Java's standard libraries to perform item existence checks.

Syntax

```
boolean exists = list.contains(item);
```

Example Usage

```java
import java.util.ArrayList;
import java.util.List;

public class ItemInListExample {
    public static void main(String[] args) {
        List<String> fruits = new ArrayList<>();

        fruits.add("Apple");
        fruits.add("Banana");
        fruits.add("Orange");

        String itemToCheck = "Banana";
        boolean exists = fruits.contains(itemToCheck);

        if (exists) {
            System.out.println(itemToCheck + " exists in the list.");
        } else {
            System.out.println(itemToCheck + " does not exist in the list.");
        }
    }
}
```

Practical Applications

1. Data Validation

When processing user input or external data, you can use item in list to validate if a specific value matches any item in a predefined list of valid values.

Part I: Learn Python

2. Filtering and Searching

item in list is invaluable when searching for specific elements in a list or filtering a list to include only items that meet certain criteria.

3. Duplicate Checking

You can use item in list to prevent duplicate entries in a list or collection. Before adding a new item, you can check if it already exists in the list.

- Tuples

Tuples are another essential data structure in Python, similar to lists but with one key difference: tuples are immutable, meaning their elements cannot be changed after creation. Tuples are often used to represent collections of related data that should remain constant throughout the program's execution.

Creating a Tuple
To create a tuple in Python, you enclose the elements in parentheses () and separate them with commas:
coordinates = (3, 4)

Accessing Tuple Elements
You can access tuple elements just like list elements, using zero-based indexing:
x = coordinates[0] # Accesses the first element (3)
y = coordinates[1] # Accesses the second element (4)

Tuples as Return Values
Tuples are often used to return multiple values from a function:
def get_coordinates():
x = 5
y = 8
return x, y

x_coord, y_coord = get_coordinates()

Here, the function returns a tuple (x, y) which is then unpacked into the variables x_coord and y_coord.

Immutable Nature

Unlike lists, you cannot modify the elements of a tuple after creation. This immutability can be useful in situations where data integrity is critical.

Common Tuple Methods

Tuples don't have many methods due to their immutability. However, there are a few methods you can use:

- len(tuple): Returns the number of elements in the tuple.
- tuple.count(item): Returns the number of occurrences of the specified item.

- tuple.index(item): Returns the index of the first occurrence of the specified item.

When to Use Tuples

Tuples are suitable for situations where you want to ensure data remains constant, such as representing coordinates, dates, or any set of values that shouldn't change during program execution. Their immutability can also be helpful for preventing accidental modifications to critical data.

In the following chapters, we'll explore more data structures like dictionaries and sets, each with its unique characteristics and applications. By understanding the strengths of each data structure, you'll have a powerful set of tools to solve a wide range of programming challenges.

- Dictionaries

Dictionaries are versatile data structures that allow you to store data in key-value pairs. Unlike sequences (lists and tuples), which use numeric indices, dictionaries use keys to access values. This makes dictionaries efficient for retrieving and organizing data.

Creating a Dictionary

To create a dictionary in Python, enclose key-value pairs in curly braces {} and separate them with commas:

```
person = {
"name": "Alice",
"age": 30,
"occupation": "Engineer"
}
```

Accessing Dictionary Values

You can access values in a dictionary by using the corresponding keys:

```
name = person["name"] # Accesses the value for the key "name" ("Alice")
age = person["age"] # Accesses the value for the key "age" (30)
```

Modifying and Adding Dictionary Entries

Dictionaries are mutable, so you can modify and add entries after creation:

```
person["age"] = 31 # Updates the value for the key "age"
person["city"] = "Paris" # Adds a new key-value pair to the dictionary
```

Common Dictionary Methods
- len(dictionary): Returns the number of key-value pairs in the dictionary.
- dictionary.keys(): Returns a list of all keys in the dictionary.
- dictionary.values(): Returns a list of all values in the dictionary.
- dictionary.items(): Returns a list of key-value tuples.

Use Cases for Dictionaries

Dictionaries are ideal for scenarios where you need to map keys to corresponding values, such as representing items in an online shopping cart, storing user preferences, or managing data with named attributes.

Part I: Learn Python

- Sets

Sets are a fundamental data structure in Python that allow you to store a collection of unique elements. In this chapter, we will explore common set methods in Python, which provide various functionalities for working with sets.

Creating a Set
To create a set in Python, enclose the elements in curly braces {}:
fruits = {"apple", "banana", "orange"}

Before we delve into set methods, let's briefly review how to create a set in Python:

my_set = {1, 2, 3}

Adding and Removing Elements
You can add elements to a set using the add() method:

fruits.add("grape") # Adds "grape" to the set

Now, let's explore the common set methods:

Common Set Methods

- len(set): Returns the number of elements in the set.

- set.add(item): Adds the item to the set.

- set.remove(item): Removes the item from the set.

- set.union(other_set): Returns a new set with elements from both sets.

- set.intersection(other_set): Returns a new set with common elements.

- set.difference(other_set): Returns a new set with elements in the current set but not in the other set.

1. len(set)
The len() method returns the number of elements in the set.
my_set = {1, 2, 3}
length = len(my_set)
print(length) # Output: 3

Part I: Learn Python

2. set.add(item)

The add() method adds the specified item to the set. If the item is already in the set, it will not be added again (since sets only contain unique elements).

```
my_set = {1, 2, 3}
my_set.add(4)
print(my_set)  # Output: {1, 2, 3, 4}
```

3. set.remove(item)

The remove() method removes the specified item from the set. If the item is not found in the set, it raises a KeyError.

```
my_set = {1, 2, 3}
my_set.remove(2)
print(my_set)  # Output: {1, 3}
```

4. set.union(other_set)

The union() method returns a new set containing all the elements from both sets without duplicates.

```
set1 = {1, 2, 3}
set2 = {3, 4, 5}
result_set = set1.union(set2)
print(result_set)  # Output: {1, 2, 3, 4, 5}
```

5. set.intersection(other_set)

The intersection() method returns a new set containing elements that are common to both sets.

```
set1 = {1, 2, 3}
set2 = {3, 4, 5}
result_set = set1.intersection(set2)
print(result_set)  # Output: {3}
```

6. set.difference(other_set)

The difference() method returns a new set containing elements that are in the current set but not in the other set.

```
set1 = {1, 2, 3}
set2 = {3, 4, 5}
result_set = set1.difference(set2)
print(result_set)  # Output: {1, 2}
```

These common set methods provide powerful tools for manipulating sets in Python and are useful in various scenarios, such as data analysis, filtering unique values, and performing set operations.

Use Cases for Sets

Part I: Learn Python

Sets are helpful for scenarios where you need to ensure uniqueness or perform set operations, such as finding common elements between two datasets, removing duplicates from a list, or checking for membership in a collection.

By understanding how to work with lists, tuples, dictionaries, and sets, you'll be equipped to handle a wide array of data manipulation tasks in Python. These data structures form the building blocks for more complex programs and algorithms, enabling you to create efficient and elegant solutions to various programming challenges.

Functions
- Defining Functions
- Parameters and Return Values
- Lambda Functions
- Scope and Lifetime of Variables

Functions are the building blocks of modular and reusable code in Python and Django. They encapsulate logic to promote code organization and facilitate the creation of maintainable applications. In this chapter, we'll delve into the world of functions, exploring how to define, call, and pass data to them. Additionally, we'll explore the concepts of function parameters, return values, and scope, allowing you to create efficient and flexible code. Understanding functions is pivotal for both Python application development and Django web development, as they enable you to structure your codebase and encapsulate business logic effectively. So, let's embark on this journey to master the art of functions and elevate your Python and Django programming skills.

Functions play a crucial role in breaking down complex tasks into manageable components. In this chapter, we'll delve into the world of functions in Python, covering Defining Functions, Parameters and Return Values, Lambda Functions, Scope and Lifetime of Variables.

-

Part I: Learn Python

- Defining Functions

In Python Django, functions play a significant role in creating views, which handle HTTP requests and generate HTTP responses. A view function in Django is essentially a Python function that performs a specific task when triggered by a URL. In this chapter, we'll explore how to define and use view functions in Python Django.

Introduction to View Function Definition

In Python Django, view functions are defined within Django apps, and they are responsible for processing HTTP requests and returning HTTP responses. Here's the basic structure of a view function definition in Django:

```python
from django.http import HttpResponse

def my_view(request):
    # Perform tasks specific to the view
    return HttpResponse("Hello, Django World!")
```

In this example, we define a view function called my_view. When this view is accessed through a URL, it returns an HTTP response with a "Hello, Django World!" message.

Using View Functions in Django

Once a view function is defined, you need to map it to a URL so that it can be accessed by clients. This mapping is typically done in Django's urls.py file. Here's how you can map a view function to a URL:

```python
from django.urls import path
from . import views

urlpatterns = [
    path('hello/', views.my_view, name='hello'),
]
```

In this example, the my_view function is mapped to the URL path 'hello/'.

Practical Applications

1. Request Handling

View functions in Django handle various HTTP methods like GET, POST, and more. They are responsible for processing incoming requests, performing tasks such as database queries, and returning appropriate responses.

Part I: Learn Python

2. Template Rendering
Django view functions can render HTML templates, allowing you to dynamically generate web pages by combining data from the database with HTML templates.

3. Authentication and Authorization
View functions can implement user authentication and authorization logic, ensuring that only authorized users can access certain parts of your web application.

Request Handling in Django View Functions
In Django, view functions play a critical role in handling incoming HTTP requests, processing data, and returning appropriate responses. This chapter explores the concept of request handling in Django and how view functions are used for this purpose.

Introduction to Request Handling
Django is a web framework designed to facilitate the development of web applications. Central to this process is the handling of HTTP requests. When a user interacts with a Django-powered website by visiting a URL or submitting a form, Django's view functions come into play. View functions are Python functions that are responsible for processing incoming requests and returning responses. They can perform various tasks, including database queries, data manipulation, and rendering templates. Django's URL routing system maps incoming URLs to specific view functions, ensuring that the appropriate function handles each request.

Key Aspects of Request Handling

1. HTTP Methods
Django view functions can handle various HTTP methods, including GET, POST, PUT, DELETE, and more. This allows for the implementation of different functionalities based on the type of request. For example, GET requests might be used for retrieving data, while POST requests can be used for submitting data to the server.

2. Database Interaction
View functions often interact with the database to retrieve, update, or manipulate data. This interaction can include querying the database for information, creating new records, or modifying existing records.

3. Rendering Responses
One of the primary responsibilities of view functions is to return responses to the client. These responses can be in various formats, such as HTML, JSON, or XML. Django provides tools to render templates, generate dynamic content, and format responses appropriately.
Practical Applications

Request handling in Django view functions is crucial for building dynamic and data-driven web applications. Here are some practical applications:

User Registration: View functions can handle user registration by processing user input, validating data, and creating user accounts in the database.

Content Management: For content-driven websites, view functions retrieve and display articles, blog posts, or other content from a database.

Authentication: View functions implement user login and logout, ensuring secure access to restricted areas of a website.

Form Processing: Forms submitted by users can be processed by view functions, validating input, saving data, and providing feedback.

we've explored the concept of request handling in Django view functions. These functions serve as the backbone of Django web applications, responsible for processing incoming HTTP requests, interacting with databases, and rendering responses. Understanding how to create and use view functions effectively is essential for building robust and feature-rich web applications with Django.

Template Rendering in Django View Functions
In Django, view functions are not only responsible for processing requests but also for rendering HTML templates. This chapter delves into the concept of template rendering in Django view functions and how it enables you to create dynamic web pages by combining data from the database with HTML templates.

Introduction to Template Rendering
Web applications often require dynamic web pages that display data retrieved from a database or generated on the server. Django's template rendering engine allows you to create HTML templates that can be populated with data and rendered as part of a response. This separation of logic and presentation is a fundamental principle of web development known as the Model-View-Template (MVT) architecture (similar to Model-View-Controller or MVC).

Key Aspects of Template Rendering

1. HTML Templates
Django templates are HTML files with placeholders (template tags) for dynamic content. These template tags are enclosed in double curly braces {{ }} and allow you to insert variables and expressions.

2. Template Context

In view functions, you create a context dictionary that contains data to be rendered in the template. This dictionary maps variable names (used in template tags) to actual data from the database or other sources.

3. Rendering Process
The rendering process involves loading an HTML template, processing template tags to replace them with data from the context dictionary, and generating the final HTML output. This output is then sent as the response to the client.

Practical Applications
Template rendering in Django is used for various purposes, including:

Displaying Database Content: View functions retrieve data from the database and pass it to templates for rendering. This is common in content management systems and e-commerce websites.

Generating Dynamic Pages: Templates allow you to create dynamic pages that display different content based on user input, database queries, or other factors.

Consistent Layout: Templates provide a way to maintain a consistent layout (header, footer, navigation) across multiple pages of a website.

Conditional Logic: Templates support conditional statements and loops, enabling you to create complex page layouts and dynamic content.

Template rendering is a fundamental aspect of Django view functions that enables you to create dynamic and data-driven web pages. By combining HTML templates with context data, you can generate user-friendly and interactive web applications. Understanding how to use templates effectively is essential for building appealing and functional web interfaces in Django.

Authentication and Authorization in Django View Functions
In Django web applications, view functions play a crucial role in implementing user authentication and authorization logic. This chapter explores the concepts of authentication and authorization in Django view functions and how they ensure secure access to specific parts of your web application.

Understanding Authentication and Authorization

Authentication:
Authentication is the process of verifying the identity of a user, typically through a combination of a username and a password. In Django, authentication is the process of determining if a user is who

they claim to be. Once a user is authenticated, Django can identify them and provide access to protected resources.

Authorization:
Authorization, often referred to as permissions, is the process of determining whether an authenticated user has the necessary rights to perform a specific action or access certain resources. Authorization ensures that users can only perform actions or access data that they are allowed to, based on their role or privileges.

Authentication and Authorization in View Functions
Django provides a built-in authentication system that includes user authentication, user management, and user sessions. View functions are responsible for implementing authentication and authorization logic to ensure that:

Only authenticated users can access certain views or perform specific actions.
Users have the appropriate permissions to access or modify specific data.

Key Aspects of Authentication and Authorization in View Functions

1. User Authentication:
Django's authentication system handles user login and user session management. View functions typically include authentication checks to ensure that users are logged in before granting access to protected views or actions.

```
from django.contrib.auth.decorators import login_required

@login_required
def protected_view(request):
    # This view is protected; only authenticated users can access it.
    ...
```

2. User Authorization:
Authorization logic is implemented within view functions to check whether a user has the necessary permissions to perform specific actions. This may involve checking the user's role, group membership, or custom permissions.

```
from django.contrib.auth.decorators import permission_required

@permission_required('app.can_edit_data')
def edit_data(request):
    # This view requires the 'can_edit_data' permission.
```

...

3. Custom Authorization Logic:
In addition to Django's built-in authorization features, view functions can implement custom authorization logic based on application-specific requirements.

Practical Applications
Authentication and authorization in Django view functions are used for various purposes, including:

User Access Control: Restricting access to certain views or actions based on user roles and permissions.

User Registration and Login: Handling user registration, login, and logout processes. Custom Permissions: Defining and managing custom permissions for specific actions or resources.

Session Management: Maintaining user sessions and managing user data while they are logged in.

Authentication and authorization are critical aspects of Django web applications that ensure secure access control and data protection. View functions are responsible for implementing these features to guarantee that only authenticated users with appropriate permissions can interact with specific parts of the application. Understanding how to use authentication and authorization effectively is essential for building secure and user-friendly web applications in Django.

In Python Django, view functions play a pivotal role in handling incoming HTTP requests from clients. These view functions are responsible for processing requests, performing tasks such as database queries, and returning appropriate responses. In this chapter, we'll delve into the details of how view functions handle different HTTP methods like GET, POST, and more in Python Django.

Introduction to Request Handling
HTTP is a stateless protocol, meaning that each HTTP request from a client to a server is independent. View functions in Django act as request handlers, providing the necessary logic to process these incoming requests and generate responses. Here's an overview of how view functions handle different HTTP methods:

- GET Requests: Typically used for retrieving data, view functions can query the database or other data sources to fetch information. The response may include HTML templates or JSON data, depending on the client's needs.

- POST Requests: Used for submitting data to the server, view functions can handle form submissions, validate data, and save it to the database. They often involve user authentication and authorization to ensure the security of the data.

- Other HTTP Methods: Django supports other HTTP methods like PUT, DELETE, and PATCH. View functions can be configured to respond to these methods as needed, allowing for a wide range of functionalities in your web application.

Example: Handling a GET Request

```
from django.http import HttpResponse

def get_example(request):
    # Logic to fetch data from the database
    data = fetch_data_from_database()

    # Return an HTML response
    return HttpResponse(data)
```

Example: Handling a POST Request

```
from django.http import HttpResponse
from django.views.decorators.csrf import csrf_exempt

@csrf_exempt
def post_example(request):
```

Part I: Learn Python

```python
if request.method == 'POST':
    # Logic to process and save data from the POST request
    save_data_to_database(request.POST['data'])

    # Return a success response
    return HttpResponse("Data saved successfully!")
else:
    # Handle other HTTP methods if needed
    return HttpResponse(status=405)  # Method Not Allowed
```

Practical Applications

1. Form Handling

View functions are commonly used for processing HTML forms submitted by users. They validate form data, handle file uploads, and store the information in the database.

2. RESTful APIs

Django view functions are ideal for building RESTful APIs that respond to various HTTP methods, allowing for the creation, retrieval, modification, and deletion of resources.

3. User Authentication

View functions can enforce user authentication and authorization, ensuring that only authorized users can access specific views or perform certain actions.

Template Rendering with View Functions in Python Django

In Python Django, view functions are instrumental in rendering HTML templates, enabling the dynamic generation of web pages by combining data from the database with HTML templates. In this chapter, we'll explore how view functions can render templates and discuss the practical applications of template rendering in Django web development.

Introduction to Template Rendering

Template rendering in Django involves the process of generating dynamic web pages by combining structured data with HTML templates. View functions play a crucial role in this process, as they retrieve data from various sources, process it, and pass it to the appropriate template for rendering. Here's an overview of how template rendering works:

A view function retrieves data from the database, performs calculations, or processes user input.

The view function selects an HTML template to render. Templates in Django use a special template language that allows for dynamic content insertion.

The view function passes the data as context to the template.

The template renders the HTML page, dynamically replacing placeholders with the data provided in the context.

The generated HTML page is sent as an HTTP response to the client's browser.

Example: Rendering a Template

```
from django.shortcuts import render

def render_example(request):
    # Retrieve data from the database or perform other operations
    data = fetch_data_from_database()

    # Pass the data to the template and render it
    return render(request, 'template_name.html', {'data': data})
```

In this example, we use the render function provided by Django to render an HTML template named 'template_name.html' and pass the 'data' variable as context.

Practical Applications

1. Dynamic Web Pages

Part I: Learn Python

Template rendering is crucial for generating dynamic web pages that display changing data, such as product listings, user profiles, or news articles.

2. Separation of Concerns
Django promotes the separation of concerns by separating the logic (in view functions) from the presentation (in templates). This separation enhances code readability and maintainability.

3. Reusable Templates
Django allows you to create reusable templates that can be shared across multiple views and applications, ensuring consistent UI elements and branding.

we've explored how view functions in Python Django can render HTML templates, enabling the creation of dynamic web pages that combine data with structured HTML. Understanding template rendering is essential for building interactive and data-driven web applications using Django. In the upcoming chapters, we'll delve deeper into Django's templating system and cover more advanced topics in web development.

User Authentication and Authorization with View Functions in Python Django
In Python Django, view functions are instrumental in implementing user authentication and authorization logic, ensuring that only authorized users can access specific parts of your web application. In this chapter, we'll explore how view functions can handle user authentication and authorization and discuss their practical applications in Django web development.

Introduction to Authentication and Authorization
Authentication is the process of verifying the identity of a user, typically through a username and password. Authorization, on the other hand, is the process of determining what actions a user is allowed to perform within the application once they are authenticated. View functions in Django play a critical role in implementing both of these processes.

Authentication:
- Verifying user credentials (e.g., username and password) during login.
- Creating user sessions to keep users logged in.
- Implementing features like "Remember Me" and "Forgot Password."

Authorization:
- Checking user roles and permissions to determine what actions they can perform.
- Restricting access to certain views or data based on user privileges.
- Implementing access control lists (ACLs) and role-based access control (RBAC) systems.

Example: User Authentication

```python
from django.contrib.auth import authenticate, login
from django.shortcuts import render, redirect

def login_view(request):
    if request.method == 'POST':
        username = request.POST['username']
        password = request.POST['password']
        user = authenticate(request, username=username, password=password)
        if user is not None:
            login(request, user)
            return redirect('dashboard')
        else:
            return render(request, 'login.html', {'error_message': 'Invalid credentials'})
    return render(request, 'login.html')
```

In this example, the login_view function handles user login. It checks the provided credentials, authenticates the user, and creates a session if the authentication is successful.

Part I: Learn Python

Practical Applications

1. Secure User Access
Authentication and authorization ensure that only authenticated and authorized users can access specific views, perform actions, or view sensitive data.

2. Role-Based Features
View functions can control which features or parts of an application are available to different user roles, such as administrators, moderators, or regular users.

3. User Data Protection
Authentication and authorization help protect user data, ensuring that users can only access their own information and cannot tamper with others' data.

we've explored how view functions in Python Django can implement user authentication and authorization logic, safeguarding your web application from unauthorized access and ensuring that users can perform actions based on their roles and permissions. Understanding these aspects of Django development is essential for building secure and user-friendly web applications. In upcoming chapters, we will dive deeper into advanced Django topics related to security and user management.

Part I: Learn Python

- Parameters and Return Values

In Python, functions are essential building blocks that often require input values, known as parameters, to perform specific tasks. They can also return values as output. This chapter provides a detailed explanation of how to define functions with parameters and return values, and how to use them effectively in your Python programs.

Defining Functions with Parameters

To define a function with parameters, you specify the parameters inside the parentheses of the function definition. Here's an example that defines a function to calculate the square of a number and takes a single parameter:

```
def square(number):
    return number ** 2
```

In this example, number is the parameter that the function square accepts.

Calling Functions with Arguments

When calling a function with parameters, you provide arguments that match the order of the parameters. For instance, to calculate the square of 5, you call the square function with an argument of 5:

```
result = square(5)
```

Return Values

Functions can return values using the return statement. The return statement specifies the value that the function sends back to the caller. In the square function example, the return statement returns the square of the input number:

```
def square(number):
    return number ** 2
```

When you call the function and store the result in a variable, you can access the returned value:

```
result = square(5)
print(result)  # Output: 25
```

Default Parameters

In Python, you can specify default values for function parameters. If a value is not provided when the function is called, the default value is used instead. This allows for greater flexibility when working with functions.

```
def greet(name="User"):
```

Part I: Learn Python

```python
return f"Hello, {name}!"
```

In this example, if you call greet() without providing an argument, it will use the default value "User."

Practical Applications
Functions with parameters and return values are used extensively in Python for various purposes, including:

- Data Transformation: Functions can accept data as parameters, perform transformations, and return the processed data.

- Modularization: Functions enable code modularization, breaking complex tasks into smaller, more manageable parts.

- Customization: Default parameters allow you to create functions that are customizable while providing sensible defaults.

- Error Handling: Functions can return error codes or messages to indicate exceptional conditions.

we've explored how to define functions with parameters and return values in Python. Understanding how to work with function parameters and return values is fundamental for creating flexible, modular, and reusable code. Python's flexibility in handling default parameters and return values makes it a powerful language for writing clean and efficient functions.

- Lambda Functions

Lambda functions, often referred to as anonymous functions, are a powerful feature in Python that allow you to create small, unnamed functions for concise and on-the-fly operations. This chapter provides a detailed explanation of lambda functions, their syntax, common use cases, and limitations.

Lambda Function Syntax
The syntax for defining a lambda function is as follows:
lambda arguments: expression

- lambda: The keyword used to declare a lambda function.

- arguments: The input parameters (arguments) that the lambda function takes.

- expression: The single expression that the lambda function evaluates and returns.

Here's an example of a simple lambda function that doubles a number:
double = lambda x: x * 2

Using Lambda Functions
Lambda functions are versatile and can be used in various scenarios:

1. Assignment to Variables
You can assign a lambda function to a variable, making it callable just like any other function:
double = lambda x: x * 2
result = double(3) # result is now 6

2. As Arguments to Functions
Lambda functions are often used as arguments to other functions, such as map(), filter(), and sorted(), where a short, simple function is required.
Example: Using map() with Lambda

numbers = [1, 2, 3, 4, 5]
doubled = list(map(lambda x: x * 2, numbers))
# doubled is now [2, 4, 6, 8, 10]

3. Sorting with Custom Key Functions
Lambda functions can define custom sorting criteria when sorting lists of objects.
Example: Sorting a List of Tuples by the Second Element

pairs = [(1, 5), (3, 1), (2, 4)]
sorted_pairs = sorted(pairs, key=lambda x: x[1])

Part I: Learn Python

sorted_pairs is now [(3, 1), (1, 5), (2, 4)]

Practical Applications
Lambda functions are commonly used for:

1. Data Transformation
They are useful for quickly transforming data by applying a simple operation to each element of a collection.

2. Filtering Data
Lambda functions can be used in conjunction with the filter() function to select elements from a collection based on specific criteria.

3. Custom Sorting
Lambda functions are valuable for custom sorting of lists or objects based on specific attributes or keys.

4. Callbacks
In libraries or frameworks that expect functions as arguments (e.g., event handlers or callbacks), lambda functions are handy for defining short, inline functions.

Limitations
While lambda functions are versatile and powerful for many purposes, they have limitations:

- Single Expression: Lambda functions can only contain a single expression. They are not suitable for complex logic or multiple statements.

- Readability: Overusing lambda functions, especially for complex operations, can reduce code readability. In such cases, defining a regular named function may be a better choice.

Lambda functions in Python are a valuable tool for creating small, anonymous functions for concise and one-time operations. By understanding their syntax, use cases, and limitations, you can leverage lambda functions to write cleaner and more efficient code in your Python programs, especially when you need short, simple functions on the fly.

-

- Scope and Lifetime of Variables

Variables created within a function are considered local variables and have limited scope within that function. They are not accessible outside the function. Here's an example that demonstrates variable scope:

```python
def example_function():
local_variable = "I am local"
print(local_variable)

example_function()
# print(local_variable) # This line would result in an error
```

The variable local_variable is confined to the scope of the example_function.

Understanding functions is a pivotal step in becoming a proficient Python programmer. They enhance code organization, reusability, and readability. As you master defining functions, handling parameters and return values, experimenting with lambda functions, and navigating variable scope, you'll gain a valuable toolkit for solving a wide range of programming challenges. In the next chapter, we'll expand on this knowledge by exploring modules and packages, further enriching your programming capabilities.

Modules and Packages
- Importing Modules
- Creating Your Own Modules
- Exploring Python Standard Library

Modules and packages are the cornerstones of code organization and reuse in Python and Django. They enable you to break your code into manageable components and share functionality across different parts of your application or even with other developers. In this chapter, we'll embark on a journey to explore the world of modules and packages. You'll discover how to create and use modules to organize your code logically, and how to leverage packages to structure your projects efficiently. This knowledge is essential for building scalable and maintainable Python applications and developing feature-rich web applications with Django. So, let's dive into the realm of modules and packages, and empower your Python and Django development endeavors.

In Python, modularization is a key principle that promotes code organization, reusability, and maintainability. By breaking down your code into smaller, manageable pieces called modules, you can build more complex programs while keeping things organized. In this chapter, we'll focus on understanding and working with modules and packages.

Part I: Learn Python

-   Importing Modules

Python provides a wide range of built-in modules that offer various functionalities. To use a module in your code, you need to import it first. Let's start with a simple example:

```python
# Import the math module
import math

# Using functions from the math module
print(math.sqrt(25)) # Calculates the square root of 25
print(math.pi) # Prints the value of pi
```

You can also import specific functions or classes from a module using the from keyword:

```python
# Importing specific functions from the math module
from math import sqrt, pi

print(sqrt(16)) # Calculates the square root of 16
print(pi) # Prints the value of pi
```

Python's strength lies in its extensive standard library, which includes a wide range of built-in modules offering various functionalities. To utilize these modules in your code, you must first import them. This chapter explains how to import modules and their specific functions or classes, enhancing your understanding of this fundamental Python concept.

Importing Entire Modules

You can import an entire module using the import keyword. Once imported, you can access its functions, classes, and variables using dot notation.

```python
# Import the math module
import math

# Using functions and constants from the math module

print(math.sqrt(25))  # Calculates the square root of 25
print(math.pi)  # Prints the value of pi
```

In this example, the math module is imported, and its sqrt() function and pi constant are used.

Importing Specific Functions or Classes

If you only need certain functions or classes from a module, you can import them explicitly using the from keyword.

```python
# Importing specific functions from the math module
from math import sqrt, pi

# Using the imported functions and constant
print(sqrt(16))  # Calculates the square root of 16
print(pi)  # Prints the value of pi
```

In this case, only the sqrt() function and pi constant from the math module are imported, making them directly accessible in your code.

Aliasing Module Names
You can provide an alias or nickname for a module to simplify its usage, especially for modules with long names.

```python
# Import the pandas module with an alias
import pandas as pd

# Using functions and classes from the pandas module using the alias
data = pd.DataFrame(...)
```

Here, the pandas module is imported with the alias pd, allowing you to use pd as a shorter reference to the module throughout your code.

Practical Applications
Importing modules is essential for extending Python's functionality and accessing pre-built solutions for various tasks, including:

- Data manipulation with modules like pandas and numpy.

- Web development with modules like flask and Django.

- Scientific computing with modules like scipy.

- File handling with modules like os and shutil.

- Working with databases using modules like sqlite3 and SQLAlchemy.

you've learned how to import modules and specific functions or classes in Python. This foundational skill allows you to harness the power of Python's extensive standard library and third-party packages, enabling you to streamline your code and build efficient and feature-rich applications.

Part I: Learn Python

- Creating Your Own Modules

Creating your own modules is a powerful way to organize your code. Suppose you have a file named my_module.py with the following content:

```
# my_module.py

def greet(name):
return f"Hello, {name}!"
```

You can import and use this module in another script:

```
import my_module

message = my_module.greet("Alice")
print(message) # Output: Hello, Alice!
```

Python's modular design allows you to create your own modules, organizing your code into reusable components. This chapter explores the process of creating your own modules and importing them into other scripts for improved code organization and maintainability.

Creating Your Own Module

To create your own module in Python, you need to create a Python file (with a .py extension) containing the functions, classes, or variables you want to encapsulate. Let's create an example module named my_module.py:

```
# my_module.py

def greet(name):
    return f"Hello, {name}!"
```

This module contains a single function, greet(), which takes a name as an argument and returns a greeting message.

Importing Your Module

Once you've created your module, you can import it into other Python scripts using the import keyword. Here's how to import and use the my_module module:

```
# Import your custom module
import my_module

# Use a function from your module
```

Part I: Learn Python

```python
message = my_module.greet("Alice")
print(message)  # Output: Hello, Alice!
```

In this example, we import the my_module module and use its greet() function to generate a greeting message.

Aliasing Module Names
Similar to importing built-in modules, you can provide an alias for your custom module to simplify its usage.

```python
# Import your custom module with an alias
import my_module as mm

# Use a function from your module using the alias
message = mm.greet("Bob")
print(message)  # Output: Hello, Bob!
```

Using an alias, such as mm in this case, makes it easier to reference your custom module throughout your code.

Practical Applications
Creating and using your own modules is valuable for:

- Code Organization: Modules help organize your code into logical components, making it more manageable as your project grows.

- Reusability: You can reuse functions, classes, or variables across multiple scripts and projects, avoiding redundant code.

- Collaboration: Modules facilitate collaboration by allowing team members to work on different parts of a project independently.

- Testing: Modules make it easier to test individual components of your code in isolation.

Creating and using your own modules is a powerful technique for organizing and structuring your Python code. By encapsulating related functionality into modules, you improve code readability, maintainability, and reusability. This practice is essential for building efficient and maintainable Python projects

- Exploring Python Standard Library

Python comes with a comprehensive collection of modules known as the standard library. These modules cover a wide range of tasks, from file handling and regular expressions to working with dates and times. Let's take a glimpse at using the random module from the standard library:

```
import random

# Generate a random integer between 1 and 10
random_number = random.randint(1, 10)
print(random_number)
```

Remember that the Python standard library is a treasure trove of tools that can simplify various programming tasks. As you become more proficient in Python, you'll find that many common functionalities are already available through these modules.

Modules and packages are foundational concepts in Python that enable you to build organized, reusable, and efficient code. Whether you're importing existing modules, creating your own, or leveraging the power of the Python standard library, mastering modules and packages will enhance your ability to create robust and maintainable programs. In the next chapters, we'll continue to explore Python's building blocks and deepen our understanding of the language's capabilities.

Python & Django

A Python framework for MTV applications

Epistle

Django Fundamentals
- What is Django?
- MVC Architecture
- Installing Django

Django, a high-level Python web framework, is renowned for its simplicity, efficiency, and robust features. In this chapter, we'll embark on a journey through the fundamental concepts of Django. You'll explore the structure of Django projects and applications, understand the Model-View-Controller (MVC) architecture, and delve into the powerful Object-Relational Mapping (ORM) system. Django's fundamentals provide the bedrock for developing dynamic web applications, enabling you to build feature-rich and scalable projects with ease. So, let's begin our exploration of Django's core principles and set the stage for crafting sophisticated web applications using this versatile framework.

- What is Django?

Django is a high-level Python web framework designed to simplify and expedite the process of building web applications. Developed with the principle of "Don't Repeat Yourself" (DRY) in mind, Django encourages efficient and reusable code. It provides a robust foundation for creating dynamic, data-driven websites by handling many common web development tasks, so developers can focus on the unique aspects of their projects.

Django encompasses several essential components, including an Object-Relational Mapping (ORM) system for database interaction, a URL dispatcher for handling URL routing, a template engine for generating HTML, and a powerful administrative interface for managing application data.

- MVC Architecture

Django follows the Model-View-Controller (MVC) architectural pattern, which promotes a clear separation of concerns within an application. However, Django's implementation has slight variations and is often referred to as Model-View-Template (MVT):

- Model: The Model handles data storage, manipulation, and retrieval. It represents the structure of the database and provides an abstraction layer over the database tables.
- View (Template): The View is responsible for presenting data to the user. In Django, it's often referred to as the Template. Templates allow you to generate dynamic HTML by combining static HTML with placeholders for data.
- Controller: The Controller in traditional MVC handles user input and directs it to appropriate components. In Django, this functionality is primarily managed by the URL dispatcher, which maps URLs to views (templates).

- Installing Django

Before diving into Django development, you need to set up your development environment, and that begins with installing Django. Here's how you can do it:

1. Virtual Environment (Optional but Recommended): It's a good practice to create a virtual environment to isolate your project's dependencies. This prevents conflicts between different projects. You can create a virtual environment using tools like venv or virtualenv.
2. Installing Django: Once you have your virtual environment set up (if you're using one), you can install Django using pip, the Python package manager. Open your terminal/command prompt and run:

pip install Django

Verification: After the installation is complete, you can verify it by running the following command:

django-admin --version

With Django installed, you're ready to start building web applications using its powerful features and conventions.

Creating a Django Project
- Setting Up a Project
- Project Structure
- Understanding Settings

Starting a new web project in Django is an exciting first step toward building feature-rich and scalable web applications. In this chapter, we'll guide you through the process of creating your first Django project. You'll learn how to set up a project environment, define project settings, and create the essential directory structure. By the end of this chapter, you'll have a solid foundation for launching your Django journey, ready to bring your web development ideas to life. So, let's begin the journey by creating your very first Django project and unlock the potential of this powerful web framework.

- Setting Up a Project

When setting up a new Django project, it's important to follow best practices to ensure a clean and organized structure. Here's a step-by-step guide:

Install Django:
If you haven't already, you need to install Django. You can use the following command:
pip install django

Create a Project:
Navigate to the directory where you want to create your project and run:
django-admin startproject projectname
This will create a new directory named "projectname" containing the initial project structure.

Virtual Environment:
It's recommended to use a virtual environment to isolate your project dependencies. Create a virtual environment:
python -m venv venv

Activate Virtual Environment:
On Windows:
venv\Scripts\activate
On macOS/Linux:
source venv/bin/activate

- Project Structure

Django enforces a specific project structure for better organization:

manage.py: A command-line utility that lets you interact with the project. You can run development server, create database tables, and more using this tool.

projectname/: This is the main project package.

- settings.py: Configuration settings for your project.
- urls.py: URL routing configuration.
- wsgi.py: Entry point for WSGI-compatible web servers.
- asgi.py: Entry point for ASGI-compatible web servers (for asynchronous code).

- Understanding Settings

The settings.py file is a crucial part of your Django project. It contains various configurations, including:

- Database Configuration: You can configure the database backend, connection details, and more. By default, Django uses SQLite, but you can use other databases like PostgreSQL, MySQL, etc.
- Installed Apps: These are the modules or apps that your project will use. Django comes with many built-in apps for common functionalities, and you can create your own apps as well.
- Middleware: Middleware components process requests and responses globally. They can be used for authentication, security, and more.
- Templates: Configure the template engine, directories for template files, and template context processors.
- Static Files: Define directories for storing static files like CSS, JavaScript, and images.
- Media Files: Specify where user-uploaded media files will be stored.
- Authentication and Authorization: Configure user authentication and authorization settings.
- Time Zone and Internationalization: Set the time zone and configure internationalization and localization settings.

It's important to carefully configure these settings to ensure your project functions correctly and securely.

Remember, a well-structured project will make it easier to collaborate, maintain, and scale your application as it grows. Following these steps and understanding the project structure and settings will set you on the right path for building a successful Django project.

Building Views and Templates
- Views and URL Mapping
- Templates and Template Language
- Displaying Dynamic Data

Views and templates are the dynamic duo at the heart of Django's powerful web application development. In this chapter, we'll delve into the art of building views and templates, exploring how they allow you to define the structure and presentation of your web pages. You'll learn how to create views that handle user requests, process data, and render templates to produce dynamic HTML content. Understanding views and templates is essential for crafting user-friendly and visually appealing web applications with Django. So, let's embark on this journey to master the creation of views and templates, unlocking the potential to deliver rich, interactive web experiences.

- Views and URL Mapping

In Django, views are Python functions or classes that process requests and return responses. They are the heart of your application's logic, handling user interactions and determining what data to present. To map URLs to views, you use the URL dispatcher.

- **URL Dispatcher:**

The URL dispatcher in Django matches incoming URLs to the appropriate view functions or classes. This is achieved through the urls.py file in your Django app.

```
from django.urls import path
from . import views

urlpatterns = [
path('home/', views.home_view, name='home'),
# ... other URL patterns ...
]
```

- **View Functions:**

A view function takes an HTTP request as input and returns an HTTP response. Inside a view function, you can retrieve data from models, perform calculations, and render templates.

```
from django.shortcuts import render

def home_view(request):
return render(request, 'home.html')
```

- **Dynamic URLs:**

You can capture dynamic values from the URL and pass them as arguments to the view function.

```
path('articles/<int:article_id>/', views.article_detail, name='article_detail')

def article_detail(request, article_id):
# ... retrieve article with article_id ...
return render(request, 'article_detail.html', {'article': article})
```

- Templates and Template Language

Templates and Template Language
Django templates are HTML files enhanced with template tags and filters, allowing you to dynamically generate content based on data from your views.

- Template Tags:
Template tags are enclosed in curly braces (
{{ }}) and allow you to output dynamic content or perform logic within your templates.
<h1>Welcome, {{ user.username }}!</h1>

- Template Filters:
Filters modify the output of template variables. They follow the variable and are separated by a pipe
(
|).
<p>{{ article.content | truncatewords:50 }}</p>

- Template Inheritance:
Template inheritance lets you create a base template with common structure and placeholders for dynamic content. Other templates can extend this base template and fill in the content.

```
<!-- base.html -->
<html>
<head>...</head>
<body>
{% block content %} {% endblock %}
</body>
</html>

<!-- article_detail.html -->
{% extends 'base.html' %}

{% block content %}
<h1>{{ article.title }}</h1>
<p>{{ article.content }}</p>
{% endblock %}
```

Part II: Django Fundamentals

- Displaying Dynamic Data

Django allows you to pass dynamic data from your views to templates for rendering.

- Context Data:

In your view functions, you can create a dictionary of data (context) that you want to pass to the template.

```
def home_view(request):
articles = Article.objects.all()
context = {'articles': articles}
return render(request, 'home.html', context)
```

- Accessing Context in Templates:

Inside the template, you can access context variables using the dot notation.

```
<ul>
{% for article in articles %}
<li><a href="{% url 'article_detail' article.id %}">{{ article.title }}</a></li>
{% endfor %}
</ul>
```

Django's view and template system forms the core of dynamic web application development. By understanding and mastering these concepts, you'll be able to create interactive and data-driven web applications with ease.

Models and Databases
- Defining Models
- Working with Databases
- Querying Data with Django ORM

Models and databases are the backbone of any data-driven web application built with Django. In this chapter, we'll dive deep into the world of models and databases, exploring how they enable you to define the structure of your data and interact with databases seamlessly. You'll learn how to create Django models to represent your application's data, set up database tables, and perform common database operations like querying and filtering data. Mastering models and databases is pivotal for building robust, data-driven web applications with Django. So, let's embark on this journey to uncover the power of models and databases, and unlock the potential to handle and manage data effectively in your Django projects.

This section is crucial in understanding how Django interacts with databases and how models are used to define the structure of your data. Let's dive into details:

-

- Defining Models

In Django, models are Python classes that define the structure of your data and how it should be stored in a database. They serve as a blueprint for creating database tables and managing the data stored within them. Each attribute of a model class represents a field in the database table. Here's a breakdown of how to define models:

1. Importing Necessary Modules: Start by importing the models module from Django. This module provides the tools you need to define your models.
2. Creating Model Classes: Define a class for each type of data you want to store. For instance, if you're building a blog application, you might have a Post model and a Comment model.
3. Defining Fields: Inside each model class, define attributes that represent the fields you want to store. These attributes are instances of various field classes provided by Django (CharField, IntegerField, DateTimeField, etc.). Each field represents a column in the corresponding database table.
4. Meta Class: Within each model class, create an inner Meta class to provide additional information about the model, such as the table name, ordering options, and more.

- Working with Databases

Django abstracts away the underlying database management system, allowing you to work with various databases (such as PostgreSQL, MySQL, SQLite) without directly interacting with SQL. To work with databases in Django:

1. Database Configuration: Set up your database connection in the project's settings file. Configure the database engine, name, user, password, and other relevant details.
2. Migrations: After defining your models, create migrations. Migrations are scripts that define how the database schema should change based on your model changes. Run python manage.py makemigrations to generate these scripts.
3. Applying Migrations: Apply migrations to update the database schema with the new changes using python manage.py migrate.

Part II: Django Fundamentals

- Querying Data with Django ORM

Django provides an Object-Relational Mapping (ORM) system that allows you to interact with your database using Python objects instead of writing raw SQL queries. The ORM provides a high-level, Pythonic interface to perform database operations:

1. Creating Objects: Use the model classes you've defined to create instances of objects that represent rows in the database table.
2. Saving Objects: After creating objects, you can save them to the database using the save() method.
3. Querying: Use the ORM's query methods to retrieve data from the database. Methods like filter(), exclude(), and get() allow you to build complex queries.
4. Updating and Deleting: Use methods like update() and delete() to modify or remove records from the database.
5. Related Objects: Define relationships between models (such as ForeignKey, OneToOneField, etc.) to establish connections between different sets of data.

Django's ORM handles many aspects of database interaction for you, including security (to prevent SQL injection), optimization, and database-specific operations.

By understanding these concepts in detail, readers will gain a solid foundation in creating models, working with databases, and querying data using Django's powerful ORM.

Forms and User Input
- Building Forms
- Handling Form Submissions
- Validating User Input

Forms are a fundamental aspect of web applications that allow users to interact with your application by providing input. In the context of Django, forms are used to collect and validate user data. Django provides a powerful form handling mechanism that helps streamline the process of creating, rendering, and processing forms.

-

- Building Forms

Building forms in Django involves defining a Python class that inherits from django.forms.Form or django.forms.ModelForm. Each field in the form corresponds to a form field class provided by Django, such as CharField, EmailField, IntegerField, etc.

Here's an example of building a simple contact form using Django's Form class:

```
from django import forms

class ContactForm(forms.Form):
name = forms.CharField(max_length=100)
email = forms.EmailField()
message = forms.CharField(widget=forms.Textarea)
```

- Handling Form Submissions

Once you've defined a form, you need to handle form submissions. When a user submits a form, the data is sent to the server for processing. In Django, you can handle form submissions in your views.

Here's an example of handling a form submission in a Django view:

```python
from django.shortcuts import render
from .forms import ContactForm

def contact_view(request):
if request.method == 'POST':
form = ContactForm(request.POST)
if form.is_valid():
# Process the valid form data here
name = form.cleaned_data['name']
email = form.cleaned_data['email']
message = form.cleaned_data['message']
# Perform further actions (e.g., sending emails)
else:
form = ContactForm()
return render(request, 'contact.html', {'form': form})
```

- Validating User Input

Django provides built-in validation for form fields. When a form is submitted, Django performs validation on each field based on the field's type and any additional validation rules you've defined.

Validation ensures that the data submitted by users is in the expected format and meets certain criteria. If validation fails, errors are attached to the form fields, and users are informed about the issues.

You can access the cleaned and validated data using the cleaned_data attribute of the form. This attribute contains a dictionary of cleaned values.

```
if form.is_valid():
name = form.cleaned_data['name']
email = form.cleaned_data['email']
message = form.cleaned_data['message']
# Process the data...
```

Django also provides customizable form field validation by adding methods to the form class with names like clean_<fieldname>().

Overall, the combination of building forms, handling submissions, and validating user input allows you to create interactive and user-friendly experiences in your Django applications. Make sure to provide clear error messages and user feedback to enhance the usability of your forms.

User Authentication and Authorization
- User Registration and Login
- User Authentication Methods
- Managing User Permissions

User authentication and authorization are paramount for securing web applications and ensuring that users can access the appropriate resources. In this chapter, we'll delve into the world of user authentication and authorization in Django, exploring how to manage user accounts, validate credentials, and enforce access control. You'll learn how to implement user registration, login, and password reset functionalities, as well as how to control user permissions and roles. Mastering user authentication and authorization is essential for building secure and user-friendly web applications with Django. So, let's embark on this journey to fortify your Django projects with robust user management features and ensure data privacy and security for your users.

- User Registration and Login:

User registration and login are fundamental aspects of any web application that requires user interaction. Here's a step-by-step breakdown of each process:

User Registration:
1. Registration Form: Provide users with a registration form where they can enter their necessary information, such as username, email, and password.
2. Data Validation: Validate user input to ensure data integrity and accuracy.
3. Password Hashing: Hash the user's password before storing it in the database to enhance security.
4. Creating User: Create a user instance in your Django application using the provided information.
5. Sending Confirmation Email: Optionally, send a confirmation email with a unique token or link to verify the user's email address.

User Login:
1. Login Form: Provide users with a login form that requires them to input their credentials (username/email and password).
2. Authentication: When a user submits their login credentials, compare them with the stored credentials in the database.
3. Session Management: If the credentials are correct, create a session for the user to keep them logged in. This can be done using Django's built-in session management features.
4. Security Measures: Implement security measures like session timeouts and CSRF protection to prevent session hijacking.

Part II: Django Fundamentals

- User Authentication Methods

Django offers various authentication methods to suit different use cases. Some common methods include:

1. Username/Password Authentication: The basic method where users log in using a combination of their username/email and password.
2. Social Authentication: Allow users to log in using their existing social media accounts (e.g., Google, Facebook, Twitter).
3. Token-Based Authentication: Provide users with tokens that they can use to authenticate their requests. This is commonly used in API authentication.
4. Multi-Factor Authentication (MFA): Enhance security by requiring users to provide additional forms of authentication, such as a verification code sent to their email or phone.

Part II: Django Fundamentals

- Managing User Permissions

User permissions dictate what actions a user can perform within the application. Django uses a permission system that allows you to define and manage user access effectively.

1. Default Permissions: Django comes with default permissions such as add, change, and delete. These permissions control users' abilities to create, modify, and delete instances of specific models.
2. Custom Permissions: You can define your own custom permissions based on your application's requirements. For example, you might create a permission that allows only administrators to publish articles.
3. Assigning Permissions: Permissions can be assigned to users individually or collectively by assigning them to groups. Groups can then be assigned to users, simplifying permission management.
4. Permission Checks: In your views or API endpoints, you can perform permission checks to ensure that only authorized users can access certain resources or perform specific actions.

Remember that the security of user authentication and authorization is of paramount importance in any application. Always follow best practices, such as using secure password hashing, protecting against common vulnerabilities like SQL injection and cross-site scripting (XSS), and staying informed about the latest security updates in Django and its dependencies.

Building a Complete Django Application
- Integrating Views, Templates, and Models
- Creating User-friendly URLs
- Adding User Authentication

Now that you've gained a solid understanding of Django's fundamentals, it's time to put your knowledge into action by building a complete Django application. In this chapter, we'll guide you through the process of creating a fully functional web application from start to finish. You'll learn how to design your application, define models, set up views and templates, handle user authentication, and connect everything together to create a seamless user experience. By the end of this chapter, you'll have a comprehensive Django application that showcases your skills in web development and serves as a valuable project in your portfolio. So, let's embark on this journey to bring your web application idea to life using the power of Django.

Let's dive into a more detailed explanation of building a complete Django application, including integrating views, templates, models, creating user-friendly URLs, and adding user authentication.

Part II: Django Fundamentals

- Integrating Views, Templates, and Models

When building a Django application, it's important to integrate views, templates, and models seamlessly to create a functional and visually appealing user experience. Here's how you can do it:

- Views: Views in Django are responsible for processing user requests and returning appropriate responses. Define views using functions or classes, and map them to URLs using the URL dispatcher. Within views, you can interact with models to retrieve data from the database and pass it to templates for rendering.

- Templates: Templates allow you to define the structure and presentation of your web pages. Django's template language enables dynamic content rendering using data from views. Templates can include placeholders for dynamic data, conditionals, loops, and template tags.

- Models: Models represent the structure of your application's data. Define models as Python classes that subclass django.db.models.Model. Each attribute of a model class corresponds to a database field. Models define relationships between data entities and provide a high-level abstraction for database interactions.

- Creating User-friendly URLs

User-friendly URLs are essential for both SEO and user experience. Django's URL dispatcher provides a way to create clean and meaningful URLs. Here's how you can achieve this:

- URL Routing: Define URL patterns in your application's urls.py file using regular expressions and route them to corresponding views. Consider using named URL patterns to make URL handling more readable.
- Slug Fields: When working with dynamic URLs, such as displaying detailed pages for each item in a database, consider using slug fields in your models. Slugs are human-readable URL fragments derived from a title or name.

- Adding User Authentication

User authentication ensures that only authorized users can access certain parts of your application. Django provides a robust authentication system that you can easily integrate:

- User Registration: Allow users to create accounts using a registration form. Collect essential user information and save it in the database using Django's built-in user model or a custom user model.
- User Login: Implement a login system where users can provide their credentials (username/email and password) to access their accounts. Django's authentication views can simplify this process.
- User Authentication Methods: Django supports various authentication methods, including session-based authentication and token-based authentication (for APIs). Choose the method that best suits your application's needs.
- Managing User Permissions: Django's permission system lets you control what users can do within your application. Define permissions and apply them to views or objects to restrict access based on user roles.

By integrating views, templates, models, creating user-friendly URLs, and adding user authentication, you'll be able to create a comprehensive Django application that provides a smooth user experience, securely manages user data, and effectively communicates with the backend. Don't forget to thoroughly test your application at each step to ensure it works as intended.

Working with Static and Media Files
- Managing Static Files
- Handling User-Uploaded Files

Static files are files that don't change and are served directly to users without any processing. These include CSS stylesheets, JavaScript files, images, and more. Django provides a built-in mechanism to manage and serve static files efficiently.

1. Static Files Configuration:
   In your Django project, you should have a directory named "static" where you can organize your static files. To configure Django to handle static files, follow these steps:
   - Add 'django.contrib.staticfiles' to your INSTALLED_APPS in the settings.py file.
   - Use the {% static %} template tag to reference static files in your templates.

2. Collecting Static Files:
   When you're ready to deploy your project, use the
   collectstatic management command. This command gathers all your static files from various locations into a single directory, making it easier to serve them efficiently with a web server like Nginx.

User-uploaded files, also known as media files, are dynamic files that can change frequently and are unique to each user. These can include images, videos, documents, and more. Django provides a convenient way to manage and serve media files.

Media Files Configuration:
Similar to static files, configure Django to handle media files by following these steps:
1. Add the following to your settings.py:
2. The MEDIA_URL is the URL prefix for media file URLs, and MEDIA_ROOT is the absolute filesystem path to the directory where media files will be stored.

User Uploads:
When users upload files through forms, Django provides the FileField and ImageField model fields to handle these uploads. You define these fields in your models to store the uploaded files.

Serving Media Files:
During development, Django can serve media files by adding the following to your project's urls.py:
In production, it's recommended to configure your web server (like Nginx or Apache) to serve media files directly for better performance and security.

File Storage:
While Django's default file storage is suitable for development, consider using a more robust storage system like Amazon S3 or Google Cloud Storage for production, especially when dealing with large-scale applications.

Remember, when dealing with user-uploaded files, security is paramount. Validate and sanitize uploaded files to prevent potential security vulnerabilities like malicious file uploads.

By understanding and implementing these practices, you can effectively manage and serve both static and media files in your Django application, ensuring a smooth user experience and optimal performance.

- Managing Static Files

1. Usage in Templates:
In your HTML templates, use the
{% load static %} template tag at the beginning to load the static template tag library. Then, you can use the {% static %} template tag to reference static files. For example:

2. Versioning Static Files:
To prevent browser caching issues when you update static files, you can use the
{% get_static_prefix %} template tag to automatically add a version string to the URLs. This is particularly useful for CSS and JavaScript files. Django will manage the versioning for you.

- Handling User-Uploaded Files

Handling User-Uploaded Files (Media Files) - Continued:

File Uploads in Forms:
To handle file uploads in forms, you need to define a form field using Django's
 FileField or ImageField. Here's an example:

Displaying Uploaded Files:
Once files are uploaded and stored, you can display them in your templates using the
 url attribute of the model's field. For example, if you have a model named Document with an
uploaded_file field, you can display it like this:

File Validation and Cleaning:
When users upload files, you can implement custom validation logic using Django's form and model
validation methods. This allows you to ensure that uploaded files meet certain criteria before being
saved. Additionally, you can implement cleaning methods to sanitize file names and perform further
checks.

Security Considerations:
Always be cautious about security when handling user-uploaded files. Consider using libraries like
 python-magic to verify the file's type before saving it. Also, configure your web server to restrict
direct access to uploaded files to prevent unauthorized access.

Scaling and Performance:
As your application grows, you might need to consider offloading media files to a dedicated storage
service like Amazon S3 or other cloud storage solutions. This reduces the load on your application
server and improves overall performance.

File Cleanup:
Implement a strategy to manage unused or expired media files. You can create management
commands or background tasks to periodically clean up old or unused files from your media storage.

By following these guidelines and best practices, you'll be able to effectively manage both static and
media files in your Django application. This not only improves the user experience but also
contributes to the security and performance of your web application.

Part II: Django Fundamentals

RESTful APIs with Django
- Introduction to APIs
- Building RESTful APIs with Django
- Consuming APIs in Your Application

In the modern web landscape, building robust and scalable RESTful APIs is a fundamental skill for web developers, and Django makes this task seamless. In this chapter, we'll delve into the world of RESTful APIs with Django, exploring how to design, develop, and deploy APIs that follow REST principles. You'll learn how to create endpoints for data retrieval, manipulation, and interaction, as well as how to handle authentication, serialization, and versioning. Understanding RESTful APIs is crucial for building dynamic, interactive, and data-driven applications that communicate effectively with client-side frameworks and mobile apps. So, let's embark on this journey to master the art of building RESTful APIs with Django and harness the power of modern web development. Let's dive deeper into the topic of RESTful APIs with Django and provide detailed explanations along with examples for each of the sections you've outlined:

Part III: Advanced Topics

- Introduction to APIs

APIs (Application Programming Interfaces) are a way for different software applications to communicate with each other. They allow you to request and exchange data between different systems. REST (Representational State Transfer) is an architectural style for designing networked applications, and RESTful APIs follow these principles. Here's a brief overview of the main concepts:

- Resources: In REST, everything is treated as a resource. A resource can be a data entity, such as a user or a product, and it's identified by a unique URL.
- HTTP Methods: RESTful APIs use HTTP methods (GET, POST, PUT, DELETE) to perform CRUD (Create, Read, Update, Delete) operations on resources.
- Stateless: Each request from a client to the server must contain all the necessary information to understand and process the request. The server doesn't store client state.

- Building RESTful APIs with Django

Django provides tools and libraries to build robust RESTful APIs quickly. The most popular package for this purpose is Django REST framework (DRF). Here's how you can create a simple RESTful API for a list of products:

- Install Django REST Framework:

```
pip install djangorestframework
```

- Create Serializers: Serializers convert complex data types, such as Django models, into native Python data types that can be rendered into JSON or other content types.

```
from rest_framework import serializers
from .models import Product

class ProductSerializer(serializers.ModelSerializer):
class Meta:
model = Product
fields = '__all__'
```

- Create API Views:

```
from rest_framework import generics
from .models import Product
from .serializers import ProductSerializer

class ProductList(generics.ListCreateAPIView):
queryset = Product.objects.all()
serializer_class = ProductSerializer
```

- Configure URLs:

```
from django.urls import path
from .views import ProductList

urlpatterns = [
path('api/products/', ProductList.as_view(), name='product-list'),
]
```

Part III: Advanced Topics

- Consuming APIs in Your Application

Once you have a RESTful API built with Django, you can consume it in your application. Here's an example of consuming the API to display a list of products in a template:

- Consuming API in Views:

```
import requests
from django.shortcuts import render

def product_list(request):
response = requests.get('http://localhost:8000/api/products/')
products = response.json()
return render(request, 'product_list.html', {'products': products})
```

- Display Data in Template:

```
<!-- product_list.html -->
<ul>
{% for product in products %}
<li>{{ product.name }} - {{ product.price }}</li>
{% endfor %}
</ul>
```

This example demonstrates how to create a simple API using Django REST framework and then consume it within a Django application to display a list of products. Of course, this is just a starting point, and you can explore more advanced features of DRF, such as authentication, pagination, and custom endpoints, based on your project's requirements.

Part III: Advanced Topics

Testing and Debugging
- Writing Unit Tests
- Using the Django Test Framework
- Debugging Techniques

Effective testing and debugging are essential skills for maintaining the reliability and robustness of your Django applications. In this chapter, we'll explore the world of testing and debugging in Django, equipping you with the tools and techniques needed to ensure your application runs smoothly. You'll learn how to write unit tests, functional tests, and integration tests to verify your code's correctness. Additionally, we'll delve into debugging strategies to identify and fix issues efficiently. Mastering testing and debugging is crucial for building and maintaining high-quality Django applications, as it helps you catch and resolve problems before they impact users. So, let's embark on this journey to become a proficient tester and debugger, ensuring your Django projects are reliable and resilient.

Part III: Advanced Topics

- Writing Unit Tests

Unit tests are a crucial part of software development that help ensure the individual components of your code are functioning correctly. In Python, you can use the built-in unittest module or Django's testing framework to write unit tests.

Example using the unittest module:

```python
import unittest

def add(a, b):
return a + b

class TestAddFunction(unittest.TestCase):
def test_add_positive_numbers(self):
self.assertEqual(add(2, 3), 5)

def test_add_negative_numbers(self):
self.assertEqual(add(-2, -3), -5)

if __name__ == '__main__':
unittest.main()
```

- Using the Django Test Framework

Django provides a powerful testing framework for testing your applications. You can write tests for models, views, forms, and more using the TestCase class provided by Django.

Example testing a Django view:

```python
from django.test import TestCase
from django.urls import reverse

class MyViewTests(TestCase):
def test_view_returns_200(self):
response = self.client.get(reverse('my-view'))
self.assertEqual(response.status_code, 200)

def test_view_displays_correct_template(self):
response = self.client.get(reverse('my-view'))
self.assertTemplateUsed(response, 'my_template.html')
```

- Debugging Techniques

Debugging Techniques

Debugging is the process of identifying and resolving issues in your code. Python provides various tools and techniques for debugging.

Example using print statements for debugging:

```python
def divide(a, b):
print(f"Dividing {a} by {b}")
result = a / b
print(f"Result: {result}")
return result


result = divide(10, 2)
```

Example using Python's built-in pdb debugger:

```python
import pdb


def calculate(a, b):
pdb.set_trace()
result = a * b
return result


result = calculate(5, 3)
```

Remember that Django provides its own debugging tools, including detailed error pages that show traceback information and variable values when an error occurs.

These examples provide a starting point for understanding testing and debugging in Python and Django. As you progress, you can explore more advanced techniques and tools to streamline your development process and create more reliable code.

Part III: Advanced Topics

Deployment and Scaling
- Preparing for Deployment
- Hosting Options
- Scaling Django Applications

Software deployment is all of the activities that make a software_system available for use. The general deployment process consists of several interrelated activities with possible transitions between them. These activities can occur on the producer side or on the consumer side or both. Because every software system is unique, the precise processes or procedures within each activity can hardly be defined. Therefore, "deployment" should be interpreted as a general process that has to be customized according to specific requirements or characteristics

- Preparing for Deployment

Before deploying a Django application to a production environment, there are several crucial steps you need to take:

1. Environment Configuration: Make sure your production environment closely resembles your development environment. This includes using the same version of Python, installing the necessary packages, and setting environment variables.

2. Security Considerations: Set up security measures like HTTPS using SSL certificates, ensuring sensitive information like secret keys and database credentials are stored securely, and implementing proper authentication and authorization mechanisms.

3. Static and Media Files: Configure your web server to handle static and media files efficiently. Use a Content Delivery Network (CDN) for improved performance and caching.

- Hosting Options

There are various hosting options available for deploying Django applications. Here are a few with examples:

1. Shared Hosting: Shared hosting platforms like Bluehost or HostGator offer cost-effective solutions for small-scale applications. They often provide one-click deployment options for Django projects.

2. Virtual Private Server (VPS): Providers like DigitalOcean and Linode offer VPS solutions where you have more control over the environment. You can install and configure your stack as needed.

3. Platform as a Service (PaaS): Platforms like Heroku or PythonAnywhere provide easy deployment options. For example, deploying on Heroku can be as simple as pushing your code to a Git repository.

4. Infrastructure as a Service (IaaS): AWS, Google Cloud, and Azure offer IaaS solutions. You can set up virtual machines, databases, and other resources as needed.

Part III: Advanced Topics

- Scaling Django Applications

As your application gains traffic, you might need to scale it to handle increased load. Here are some scaling strategies:

1. Vertical Scaling: Increase the resources (CPU, RAM) of your server. For example, if you're using a cloud provider, you can resize your virtual machine to a more powerful instance.

2. Horizontal Scaling: Add more servers to distribute the load. Implement load balancing to evenly distribute incoming requests across multiple servers.

3. Database Scaling: Consider using database replication or sharding to manage database load. This involves distributing the database across multiple servers.

Example: Let's say you have a Django e-commerce website that's experiencing increased traffic. To scale horizontally, you can set up a load balancer that distributes incoming requests to multiple instances of your Django application. These instances can be hosted on different servers. Additionally, you can set up a replicated database to ensure data consistency across instances.

Remember, scaling requires careful planning and testing to ensure your application remains stable and responsive under increased load.

By providing detailed explanations and practical examples for each of these aspects, you'll help your readers understand the intricacies of deploying and scaling Django applications effectively. This will empower them to confidently take their projects from development to production.

CONCLUSION

Congratulations on completing the journey through "Python101 - Learning Python & Django within Hours." You've gained a solid foundation in both Python programming and Django web development. As you reflect on your journey, remember that learning is a continuous process, and this book is just the beginning.

You've covered everything from the fundamentals of Python syntax to building dynamic web applications using Django. Through hands-on examples and exercises, you've explored Python's capabilities and how they translate into powerful web solutions with Django's framework.

Next Steps:

As you move forward in your Python and Django journey, consider the following steps:

1. Build Projects: Apply what you've learned by building your projects. Practice is essential for deepening your understanding and gaining confidence.
2. Contribute to Open Source: Explore open-source Python and Django projects. Contributing to such projects is a great way to learn from experienced developers and give back to the community.
3. Dive Deeper: There's always more to learn. Explore advanced topics like asynchronous programming, Django REST framework for APIs, and more.
4. Stay Updated: Technology evolves quickly. Keep up with the latest Python and Django updates, trends, and best practices.
5. Engage with the Community: Join online forums, social media groups, and attend meetups or conferences to connect with fellow developers. Sharing knowledge and experiences can be incredibly enriching.

Resources

Here are some resources to continue your learning journey:

1. Online Tutorials and Documentation:
   - Python Official Documentation: https://docs.python.org/
   - Django Official Documentation: https://docs.djangoproject.com/
2. Community and Forums:
   - Stack Overflow (https://stackoverflow.com/) for programming questions.
   - Reddit communities like r/learnpython and r/django.
3. Conferences and Meetups:
   - Look out for local and global Python and Django events where you can learn and network.
4. Blogs and Websites

Remember, learning programming and web development is a journey that requires patience, practice, and persistence. Embrace challenges, seek help when needed, and celebrate your successes along the way. Your newfound skills in Python and Django open up a world of possibilities, from building your projects to contributing to exciting software development endeavors. Best of luck on your continued journey!

REVISION

Other books from Tehzeeb School written by Dipesh Bhoir

Tehzeeb School

Developer CheatSheet for Python

In case you're an experienced developer with hold on other languages and frameworks, developer cheat sheets are a great way to jumpstart a topic. We are sharing a comprehensive list of topics you need to go through to reach the same stage with the Python language and Django framework.

Stage I: Python Basics

Getting Started with Python
- History of Python
- Installing Python
- Your First Python Program
- Understanding the Python Interpreter

Variables and Data Types
- Naming Variables
- Numeric Data Types (int, float)
- Text Data Type (str)
- Boolean Data Type (bool)
- Type Conversion

Operators and Expressions
- Arithmetic Operators
- Comparison Operators
- Logical Operators
- Operator Precedence

Control Flow
- Conditional Statements (if, elif, else)
- Loops (for, while)
- Control Flow Examples

Data Structures
- Lists
- Tuples
- Dictionaries
- Sets

Functions
- Defining Functions

- Parameters and Return Values
- Lambda Functions
- Scope and Lifetime of Variables

Modules and Packages
- Importing Modules
- Creating Your Own Modules
- Exploring Python Standard Library

Stage II: Django Fundamentals

Introduction to Django
- What is Django?
- MVC Architecture
- Installing Django

Creating a Django Project
- Setting Up a Project
- Project Structure
- Understanding Settings

Building Views and Templates
- Views and URL Mapping
- Templates and Template Language
- Displaying Dynamic Data

Models and Databases
- Defining Models
- Working with Databases
- Querying Data with Django ORM

Forms and User Input
- Building Forms
- Handling Form Submissions
- Validating User Input

User Authentication and Authorization
- User Registration and Login
- User Authentication Methods

- Managing User Permissions

Building a Complete Django Application
- Integrating Views, Templates, and Models
- Creating User-friendly URLs
- Adding User Authentication

Working with Static and Media Files
- Managing Static Files
- Handling User-Uploaded Files

Stage III: Advanced Topics

RESTful APIs with Django
- Introduction to APIs
- Building RESTful APIs with Django
- Consuming APIs in Your Application

Testing and Debugging
- Writing Unit Tests
- Using the Django Test Framework
- Debugging Techniques

Deployment and Scaling
- Preparing for Deployment
- Hosting Options
- Scaling Django Applications

This cheat sheet covers a wide range of topics from Python basics to building web applications using the Django framework. Make sure to tailor the content to match your target workflow and the goals of your day job. Best of luck!

By Dipesh Bhoir

Tehzeeb School
Handwritten from 2022 to 2024 in Mumbai, India.

ALL RIGHTS RESERVED
FOR BUSINESS ENQUIRY CONTACT US ON
ask@DipeshBhoir.com

Amazon Exclusive

Python101 - Learning Python & Django within hours

Happy Learning!

Printed in Great Britain
by Amazon